THE CRAFTER'S GARDEN

by Joni Prittie

THE CRAFTER'S GARDEN

by Joni Prittie

Meredith® Press
New York

A WORD FROM MEREDITH ® PRESS

All of us at Meredith ® Press are dedicated to offering you, our customer, the best books we can create. We are particularly concerned that all of our instructions for making projects are clear and accurate. Please address your correspondence to Customer Service Department, Meredith® Press, Meredith Corporation, 150 East 52nd Street, New York, NY 10022.

If you would like to order additional copies of any of our books, call 1-800-678-2803 or check with your local bookstore.

Author and Designer:
Joni Prittie,
Aptos, CA

Photography:
Todd Tsukushi,
Santa Cruz, CA, with the exception of pages 6-7, 8, 11, 12, 17, 19, 20, 35, 36, 41, 43, 45, 49, 52, 115, 118, and 168, which are by Joni Prittie

*Photostyling and
Book Packaging:*
Prittie Design,
Aptos, CA

Graphics:
Irene Morris,
Morris Design,
Monterey, CA

Illustrations:
Joni Prittie and Mike Prittie

Meredith ® Press is an imprint of Meredith ® Books:

President, Book Group:
Joseph J. Ward

Vice-President, Editorial Director:
Elizabeth P. Rice

For Meredith ® Press:
Executive Editor:
Maryanne Bannon

Associate Editor:
Carolyn Mitchell

Copy Editor:
Carol Anderson

Production Manager:
Bill Rose

Cover Photograph:
Joni Prittie

ISBN: 0-696-02382-2

Library of Congress Catalog Card Number: 93-077253

Printed in the United States of America

10 9 8 7 6 5 4 3

ACKNOWLEDGEMENTS

Whether welcoming spring or recalling the last scents of summer, you're sure to find enjoyment in the lasting pleasure of floral crafts.

We at Meredith® Press strive to bring you high-quality craft books with original designs and easy-to-follow instructions and diagrams. Each project in *The Crafter's Garden* is photographed in full color and enhanced by Joni Prittie's watercolor renderings of her own ever-evolving garden.

We hope that before you put your garden to bed this year, you'll look to this book for a fulfilling pursuit that never goes out of season.

Sincerely,

Maryanne Bannon

Maryanne Bannon
Executive Editor

Many, many thanks to the loyal, talented team who kept spirits jolly and gave talent, time, and humor to all our tasks and their attention to so many details.

Infinite gratitude to Ceci, friend and assistant, for many hours and great encouragement.

For patience and flawless photography, thanks to Todd Tsukushi. Every time we work together, the images from my imagination are transformed into film.

Tremendous thanks to Jodee Risney for her design talent, assistance in photostyling, and unwavering enthusiasm.

A special thank you to Irene Morris for many long hours of great graphic work.

To all at Meredith who made this book possible, my deep appreciation. To Maryanne Bannon, my editor, a special thanks.

Heartfelt gratitude to all those who helped me along my gardening path—my father, who dug up the plot for my first marigolds, and my mother, who sends cuttings, advice, and love.

Endless thanks to Mike, who has lived with flowers drying everywhere and ribbons draped over every chair. Thank you to Arin, my dear sister, for keeping me on track and always believing.

Wisteria Antiques once again graciously opened its doors, providing French accessories and beautiful rooms in which to film. Many thanks! And for the open door to film in a most special red log house, thanks to Cadillac Mountain Farm.

The support of suppliers has been especially encouraging. Special props and supplies have truly made the difference in creating images for *The Crafter's Garden*.

My favorite lead squirrel sculpture graces several photos thanks to Florentine Craftsmen, Inc. For those difficult-to-find English garden trugs, thank you to The British Accent.

Gratitude also to Sandy Cashman of Fiskars, Diane Carrol at Pierre Deux, Frank Forshage from Westpoint Pepperell, Elizabeth Phinder from Kaufman, and Clare Gallagher.

Once again, great thanks to gracious Paulette Knight for her wonderful French wired ribbon and enthusiastic support.

Lastly, a note of thanks and love to Ann, Susan, Karyn, Philippa, Sharon, Hattie, Karen, Penney, Allison, Christine, Ruthie, Kathy, Elizabeth, Gerda, Laurel, Nancy, Rosie, and Linda for years of love, friendship, and their unconditional encouragement.

TABLE OF CONTENTS

For Mamie, Emma, Arin, and Mike and all
who love to garden.

INTRODUCTION

It begins differently for each gardener: a few marigolds grown in orange-juice tins while in kindergarten, a tour of a famous garden in later years, or perhaps the gift of a potted rose from a dear friend. Once the universal language of flowers is spoken, the response is a lifelong friendship with plants.

Flowers and herbs fit into our lives no matter where we live. When our space is limited, a few pots of pansies or scented geraniums fill the need. Rooms come alive when a topiary or a wreath of sunny yellow daisies is introduced. Each time we grow and gather flowers, we join in the timeless traditions of all plant lovers. Each time a tree is planted, we help heal our planet. When we teach our children how to garden, we pass on the gift of finding inner peace in a hectic world.

For me gardening and crafting from the garden began at an early age as I made crowns of daisy chains and fairy skirts of petunias turned upside down. Gardening in the Midwest and along the West Coast introduced me to many varieties of flowers and herbs. The years spent gardening in England opened the door to another world of gardening...the true cottage garden. It is the love of tending plants and crafting with flowers that inspired this book.

Advice and tips from fellow gardeners, the heritage of my family's love of the land, and experimenting with craft ideas have all played a part in creating the projects in *The Crafter's Garden*.

My intention in writing this book is to share more than the basics of growing and crafting. I wish to invite you to explore the peace and creativity found in a garden. My favorite quotes and plant lore combine with the delights of making beautiful things from materials gathered just outside the door. You will find a crafter-friendly Resource Guide on page 162, with suppliers ready to help with garden and craft needs.

The projects were created with love and are meant to speak to both crafters who have a taste for traditional florals and to those who like surprises. The fairy sachet doll has a lamp made out of a dried daffodil wired with a dollhouse bulb that can really be lit.

My fondest thought is that we are neighbors trading cuttings and tips over the garden wall. *The Crafter's Garden* is every garden, for each flower is useful for crafting and each season offers botanical delights.

May you find great joy in your garden.

Joni Prittie

THE CRAFTER'S GARDEN

When we travel far to visit a classic garden of great beauty,
the inspiration of a gardener's vision is truly felt. Flowers carefully selected
for the landscape bloom in perfect time with the seasons.
And on the way to this garden, if we are very fortunate,
we shall pass by a field of wildflowers.

ardens are very personal places. Shaped by a gardener's taste for color and form and filled with favorite friends and a few surprises, a garden takes on a bit of the personality of its caretaker.

Growing a well-kept garden requires an initial investment of time and care. As plants become established, however, the reward of baskets filled with herbs and flowers, cuttings to share with friends, and vases overflowing with roses becomes an everyday blessing.

Crafting from the garden adds another dimension: there are so many easily grown plants that are useful in fashioning wreaths, garlands and gifts. With a little planning, your garden can be tailored to your crafting needs. From early spring until the garden is put to bed in the fall, flowers and leaves, branches and pods will be available for projects and potpourri.

Perennial plants offer materials year after year. Annuals and biennials are equally valuable and can be planted to fill spaces among perennial plants for color and weed control. Once a garden begins to incorporate special plants for crafting, more and more projects come to mind. Harvesting bundles of sweet herbs creates a wonderful sense of well-being; the growing and using of plants places us in an intimate cycle with nature.

Almost every plant is useful for crafting. Press forget-me-nots, dry magnolias in a desiccant, tie violets in blue ribbons, and save rose petals for winter potpourri mixtures. There are far more plants to craft with than those that appear on the following list. These are tried-and-true, and should grow well for you. Always check with your local garden shop or consult a gardening encyclopedia for plants that grow best in your climate zone.

Often plants that are not suitable for a particular climate zone can be treated as annuals and brought in potted to a sheltered position, such as a shed or garage, to winter over.

Herbs

The term herb has evaded an exact definition for almost as long as herbs have been cultivated. For classification here, they are defined as plants traditionally used for culinary and medicinal purposes. Most herbs are highly aromatic. Their value in a crafter's garden includes use in potpourris, wreaths, garlands, nosegays, and arrangements. Sprigs of herbs can be pressed and used to create pressed herbal wreaths.

RECOMMENDED PLANTS

For a Crafter's Garden

COMMON NAME:	DESCRIPTION:	GROWING TIPS:	HARVESTING AND PRESERVING:
ARTEMISIA-*all varieties* *Latin name: Artemisia compositae* *Hardy deciduous subshrub*	Many varieties are aromatic, have silver-gray or white foliage, some with small yellow or gold flowers.	Drought-resistant artemisia requires light, dry, well-drained soil and full sun. It is a good plant for a mid-border spot.	Gather leaves and flowering tops in mid to late summer. Dry leaves and flowers by hanging upside down. Use for making wreath bases and adding to arrangements.
BABY'S BREATH *Latin name: Gypsophila paniculata* *Hardy perennial*	Baby's breath lends an airy feeling to the flower bed as well as to any project where a sweet, graceful look is desired.	Plant in mid-border among colorful flowers or near roses for delightful effects. Baby's breath prefers a well-drained chalky soil and full sun.	Cut when in full flower but before white flowers begin to fade to brown. Hang upside down in small bunches to avoid tangled and broken flowers when dry.
CALENDULA/POT MARIGOLD *Latin name: Calendula officinalis* *Hardy annual*	Calendula is popular in gardens because of its cheery bright orange color and its versatility. It grows to a height of 12 to 20 inches and is good to plant toward the front of the border or mid-border.	Calendula grows well in fine loam with lots of sun but also does well in any soil that is not waterlogged. Average watering will suffice.	It is best to pick the flowers when they first open. Hang flowers upside down to air-dry petals. Dried calendula petals retain their color and are a wonderful addition to potpourri.
CARNATION/PINK *Latin name: Dianthus caryophyllus* *Hardy perennial* *Half-hardy annual/biennial*	Highly scented of cloves, plants grow in compact clumps that are best planted near the front of a bed or border. This flower has an enormous range of colors.	Plants like fertile soil and regular feeding. Full sun will help them flourish.	Cut flower heads when they are fully open and dry at once in silica gel to preserve form and color. Air-drying will produce shriveled flower heads. Reds hold their color best when dry. Small pinks dry well, and all provide individual petals for potpourri.
COCKSCOMB *Latin name: Celosia argentea cristrata* *Half-hardy annual*	Cockscomb can be grown as a potted plant as well as in the garden. Deep, velvety-red flower heads add richness to winter projects.	Sow directly in very sheltered positions or purchase plants in the spring. It is tolerant of most soils and will thrive with average watering.	Cut when in full flower, but do not strip away leaves. Hang upside down to air-dry. Use it in wreaths and arrangements.

COMMON NAME:	DESCRIPTION:	GROWING TIPS:	HARVESTING AND PRESERVING:
CORNFLOWER *Latin name: Centaurea cyanus* *Half-hardy annual*	Intense blue, pink, and white many-petaled flowers are held upright on straight stems. This flower is often found in Tudor gardens.	Sow in full sun in spring. Plants grow tall and may need support. Cut flowers all summer to ensure continual bloom. Easily grown, cornflowers tolerate average soil and moderate watering.	Cut as flowers open fully. Air-dry by hanging upside down. The bright blue cornflower holds perfect color when dried and is useful for adding flair to a potpourri or any project that requires a vivid blue.
DELPHINIUM *Latin name: Delphinium elatum* *Deciduous perennial*	For lovers of blue flowers, there is none more beautiful than the delphinium. Available in every shade from pale sky-blue to the deepest midnight blue, it adds wonderful nuances of tone to every craft project.	Full sun or partial shade is best for most varieties. A rich, deeply-dug, well-drained soil will produce the best blooms. Provide support for tall flower spikes. It should be grown toward the back of a border or bed.	Cut when almost all flowers are open on a spike. Air-dry spikes or dry individual flowers in silica gel for perfect form and color.
FORGET-ME-NOT *Latin name: Myosotis sylvatica* *Perennial*	The forget-me-not has oblong, tapered leaves and small blue flowers. It grows to a height of 12 inches and is good as a border. Forget-me-nots bloom in mid to late spring.	Forget-me-nots need moist, well-drained soil in partial shade. The soil should not be allowed to dry out. Plant throughout the garden for blue accents.	Flowers and leaves are good for pressing and can be dried in silica gel for delicate projects.
GLOBE AMARANTH *Latin name: Gomphrena globosa* *Half-hardy annual*	An everlasting, it grows from 12 to 18 inches, producing cloverlike flowers of magenta, red, and creamy white with a papery texture.	Plants are placed out in spring and are best grown toward the front of a bed. They tolerate average soil and watering.	Globe amaranth, hung upside down, air-dries quickly. It is useful in all dried-flower projects but is too thick for pressing.
HEATHER *Latin name: Calluna vulgaris* *Evergreen shrubs*	Summer and autumn flowering varieties of heather are available in pink, cerise, and white. They should be grown near the front of a border.	Heather thrives in full sun in sandy, well-drained soil. Average watering is needed.	Because heather dries beautifully, simply use it fresh and allow it to dry in an arrangement or wreath.
HYDRANGEA *Latin name: Hydrangea macrophylla* *Deciduous shrub*	Large flower heads bloom in ball shapes on this shrub, which can grow quite tall.	The color is created largely by the type of soil in which the plant grows: pink or lime in alkaline soils, blue in acidic or clay soil. To alter flower color from pink toward the blue range, feed with additives containing iron and aluminum. If grown in the shade, flowers may have a green tint. Moist soil in a protected area or partial sun will establish healthy plants. Must be well watered during hot weather. Feed plants with compost dressings.	Cut flowers when mature (they feel papery and dry), before any frost has reached them. Hang upside down and air-dry. Hydrangea is perfect for wreaths and large arrangements when used as an entire flower head. Individual florets lend texture and interest in smaller projects.

COMMON NAME:	DESCRIPTION:	GROWING TIPS:	HARVESTING AND PRESERVING:
LARKSPUR *Latin name: Delphinium consolida* *Annual*	Pink, white, lilac, or deepest blue-purple flowers bloom on tall, slender stems.	Sow in spring, in mid-border position, because spikes grow to a height of about 3 feet. Larkspur likes a sunny place; and average soil and water will suffice.	Cut when half of the flowers are open on a spike. This will ensure open flowers for color and delicate buds at the tip. Dry by hanging upside down in bunches. Flowers may be used on the long stem or individually.
LAVENDER *Latin name: Lavandula spica* *Evergreen shrub*	A craft garden is not complete without at least one variety of lavender. Hidcote is especially deep in color and has a very pleasing fragrance. Pink and white lavenders are well worth adding to the garden for beautiful spots of color.	Lavender responds well to full sun and well-drained soil. A low hedge or border of lavenders along walkways and encircling beds works well. Be sure not to overfeed.	Cut flower stems just before buds open on spike. Hang upside down to air-dry. It is useful for all projects, especially potpourri crafting.
LOVE-IN-A-MIST *Latin name: Nigella damascena* *Hardy annual*	Love-in-a-mist is a fine blue flower for drying. It is also available in pink and in a perfect white for summer projects. Miss Jekyll is an excellent choice for blue flowers. Seedpods are round with maroon stripes.	Sow in autumn for an early summer bloom. Spring sowing will produce flowers later in the season. Love-in-a-mist will self-seed freely and does well in full sun and average soil with average watering. It is a perfect mid-border choice because it grows to a height of $1\frac{1}{2}$ to 2 feet.	Both flowers and seedpods are useful for projects. Flowers can be hung to dry, but the petals are delicate. Dried in silica gel, the flowers will retain both shape and color. Seedpods should be collected when stripes of color begin to show. Stripes will fade if the pods are left too long. This flower is useful in all craft projects and presses well.
PANSY *Latin name: Viola tricolor* *Annual*	The pansy grows to 15 inches in height and produces flowers that display the predominate patterns of purple, white, yellow, and orange. Leaves are generally heart-shaped and bright green.	Pansies may be grown in pots or toward the front of a border or bed. They like a bit of shade from the midday sun and deep watering. Keep blooms picked to encourage continual growth.	Pansies should be picked when flowers are open. They may be pressed or preserved in silica gel.
PEONY *Latin name: Paeonia* *Deciduous perennial*	Even the smallest garden can accommodate a peony, which has full, blousy blooms of heavenly color. All colors dry well, but Rubra pelna retains a gorgeous red for winter arrangements. Check with the grower for blooming times of individual varieties.	Rich, deeply-dug soil in partial or full sun suits the peony. A sheltered position is best. Water peonies well. Once established do not transplant, as peony roots do not like to be disturbed.	When harvesting single peonies, allow the flower to open and reveal the center. Cut before the petals reflex. Flowers may be hung upside down to air-dry or desiccant-dried for perfect preservation. Double peonies should be cut when outer petals and center petals are open and stamen is visible. If outer petals have turned under, it is too late. Desiccant drying assures a perfect flower for wreaths and large arrangements.

COMMON NAME:	DESCRIPTION:	GROWING TIPS:	HARVESTING AND PRESERVING:
QUEEN ANNE'S LACE *Latin name: Daucus carota* *Biennial*	Queen Anne's lace is a plant of white flower clusters, each cluster composed of approximately 500 flowers with a tiny deep-red or purple center. Leaves are feathery and fernlike.	Easy to grow toward the back of a border or bed, this plant will tolerate average to poor soil and reseed freely. Average watering and full sun will suit Queen Anne's lace.	Harvest flower heads before they begin to fade. They are good for pressing and can be silica-dried, though flower heads are delicate and require gentle handling.
ROSE *Latin name: Rosa* *Perennial shrub/climber*	Rose varieties are many. Older varieties are excellent to grow for fragrance. Hybrid and newer varieties produce perfectly shaped blooms in a vast range of colors. Available in every size from miniature to large shrub and climbing varieties, all roses are beautiful and well worth growing. Miniature roses can be grown in pots when space is limited.	Generally, well-dug, rich soil is a good beginning for roses of all varieties. Culture advice for your rose varieties can be provided by the experts at your garden center. Full sun and deep watering are generally advised.	Roses, collected at all stages, saved fully open and fading, are excellent for desiccant drying and air-drying. Choose the size of the rose according to the project. When roses are fully open, they have a better shape for air-drying. With desiccant or air-drying techniques, dry an adequate amount of rose leaves to be used in arrangements and wreaths. Almost every variety of rose produces blossoms to dry and leaves to press. Roses are the mainstay of potpourri crafting and wreath making.
SCABIOUS, PINCUSHION FLOWER *Latin name: Scabiosa dipsaceae* *Annual and perennial*	This is a personal favorite because of the lavender-blue flowers of beautiful form. White and cream varieties are equally lovely. Butterflies seem to love them. Plant in front of borders. Plants, once established, will spread to create low mounds covered with flowers. Seed heads form round textural balls.	Plant scabious in the spring in ordinary soil and water moderately. Each plant will produce many blooms that should be cut often to enable the plant to produce more.	Cut fully opened flowers for desiccant drying or harvest round seed heads after petals have dropped. Seed heads are good for autumn projects. Desiccant-dried scabious is a wonderful addition for arrangements that require blue and lavender colors.
SEA LAVENDER *Latin name: Limonium latifolium* *Hardy perennial*	This plant consists of fine, delicate flowers on airy stems that can grow to a height of 2 feet. The flowers are violet blue.	Sea lavender flourishes in full sun and dry locations. Average watering is sufficient. Plant mid-border or in front area of beds.	For best color, cut when tiny flowers are fully opened. Air-dry by hanging upside down, or use fresh and allow stems to dry in arrangements. They are useful for fillers and in delicate projects.
STATICE *Latin name: Limonium sinuatum* *Summer annual*	Statice is surprisingly easy to grow and is available in peach and antiqued pastels as well as white, blue, violet, pink, and yellow. Yellow statice seems to be a more brittle flower head than other colors. Plants grow to a height of 2 or more feet.	A native to the Mediterranean region, statice loves full sun and dry locations. Plant it mid-border for best results.	Naturally papery and dry to the touch, flowers are best cut when fully open. To ensure maximum retention of color, air-dry in a dark area. Bunch stems loosely to avoid tangling flowers. They are useful in all floral crafts.

COMMON NAME:	DESCRIPTION:	GROWING TIPS:	HARVESTING AND PRESERVING:
STRAWFLOWER *Latin name: Helichrysum bracteatum* *Half-hardy annual*	The strawflower is the best-known everlasting and is available in a wide range of autumnal colors as well as pink and white. It retains color perfectly. Double varieties are good choices for wreath and topiary projects.	This plant responds well to full sun and well-drained soil with average watering. Grow it mid-border for taller varieties. Place dwarf varieties near the front.	Cut in the morning as flowers begin to open. If the outer petals are open and center petals are still in bud form, they will continue to open after cutting and result in perfectly formed flowers. Once the main, center flower of a stalk has been cut, the side shoots will produce more blooms. Hang upside down to air-dry. It is useful in all floral projects.
SUNFLOWER *Latin name: Helianthus annus* *Tender annual*	Sunflowers grow to a height of 3 to 10 feet and are a wonderful focal point for a garden. Large flowers of bright yellow and gold follow the path of the sun during the day. Varieties include variegated browns and yellows and multipetaled types.	Sunflowers grow in any well-drained loam with a sunny location. Average watering and room in which to grow are required.	Cut flowers when fully open but before flower heads begin to fade and droop. Petals press well. Hang flowers to air-dry or preserve in silica gel.
TANSY *Latin name: Tanacetum vulgare* *Hardy herbaceous perennial*	Tansy has mustard-yellow, flat clusters that retain their color well. The plants grow to a height of 5 feet and are good planted mid-border or toward the back of beds.	Tansy grows in any soil that is not too wet and needs either full sun or light shade.	Gather flowers when open and hang upside down to air dry. They are useful in potpourri, wreaths, and other craft projects.
VIOLET *Latin name: Viola odorata* *Hardy perennial*	The violet has either white or purple blossoms with a light fragrance. Parma violets are renowned for their strong, sweet scent used in perfumes. It grows to a height of 4 to 6 inches and makes a very good ground cover.	Violets grow well in rich, moist soil with partial shade. Early-morning or late-afternoon sun is beneficial.	Gather flowers when they have opened. They may be pressed or dried in silica gel. They are useful for small, delicate projects.
YARROW *Latin name: Achillea filipendulina* *Deciduous perennial*	Yarrow is easily grown and is dependable for drying. Flat, bright flower heads measure 3 to 4 inches across and are formed on strong, straight stems. Gold plate is especially colorful.	Plants form a large clump and like full sun. Tolerant of most soils, yarrow will grow well toward the back of a border or along a wall.	Cut stems when individual florets of flower head are fully open. Hang bunches to air-dry. Use in wreaths and arrangements.
YARROW *Latin name: Achillea millefolium,* *all varieties* *Deciduous perennial*	Soft pastels and intense colors are available in the achilleas. Fern-like leaves and delicate flat flower heads grow to a height of 12 to 24 inches. Paprika has red florets with bright-yellow centers. Cerise queen is deep magenta.	Tolerant of most soils, it often prefers a bit of sand added. Plant near the front of a border or along the garden walk. Average watering will suffice.	Cut throughout the gardening season as flowers come into bloom. Air-dry by hanging in bunches. This plant is useful for wreaths and arrangements.

RECOMMENDED HERBS

For a Crafter's Garden

COMMON NAME:	DESCRIPTION:	GROWING TIPS:	HARVESTING AND PRESERVING:
BERGAMOT (BEE BALM) *Latin name: Monarda didyma* *Hardy herbaceous perennial*	A native North American plant, bergamot has several varieties that grow to a height of 2 to 3 feet and can have scarlet, soft pink, or purplish blossoms. The leaf is toothed, red-veined and exudes a strong scent.	Bergamot grows well in rich, light, moist soil with full sun (partial shade in a hot climate). A mulch should be added in the spring. Plants require average watering.	Collect leaves in spring and summer, when flowers form and scent is strong. Gather flowers when they have opened. Air-dry by hanging upside down. Flowers are good in potpourri; leaves can be used for teas and potpourri.
FEVERFEW *Latin name: Matricaria eximia* *Half-hardy annual*	The individual flowers, grown on large sprays of blossoms, resemble tiny white chrysanthemums. Feverfew opens as a creamy white flower.	Once established, feverfew seeds freely and returns each spring. Growing to a height of up to 3 feet, it is an excellent mid-border choice. Feverfew tolerates average soil and watering.	Cut when blossoms are fully open. Hang upside down to air-dry. Useful for wreaths and as a filler flower in arrangements.
HYSSOP *Latin name: Hyssopus officinalis* *Hardy semi-evergreen subshrub*	Hyssop grows to a height that ranges from 18 inches to 4 feet and has lovely pink, purple, white, or blue flowers. It works well planted mid-border. Hyssop attracts bees and butterflies in the garden.	Hyssop grows well in light, well-drained, alkaline soil with full sun. Average watering is necessary.	Flowers and budding tops should be picked as flowering begins. Leaves may be harvested at any time. Preserve hyssop in silica gel or hang upside down to air-dry. Dried, it is a wonderful addition to potpourri.
LAVENDER COTTON *Latin name: Santolina chamaecyparissus* *Evergreen small shrub*	Silver or green foliage varieties form dense clumps above which tall stems rise with bright, button-shaped yellow flowers.	Warm, sunny positions with slightly sandy, well-drained soil yield long-lived, dependable blooms. Average watering is necessary. Plant in front of a bed or mid-border.	Cut when flowers are fully open and hang upside down to dry. Hang bunches of leaves, or press individual leaves for projects.

COMMON NAME:	DESCRIPTION:	GROWING TIPS:	HARVESTING AND PRESERVING:
LEMON VERBENA *Latin name: Aloysia triphylla* *Half-hardy shrub*	Lemon verbena is known for the clean, lemony fragrance of its leaves. The plant has long, pointed leaves grouped in threes on the stem. The flowers are tiny white and light purple panicles near the top of the stem. Plants grow to a height of 2 to 4 feet in temperate climates and much higher in hot climates.	Lemon verbena likes light, well-drained, alkaline soil, but poor soil produces hardier plants that are able to survive cold winters. Plant lemon verbena in full sun and where it will be sheltered from frost. Plants may be grown in pots and brought indoors in colder climate areas.	The leaves can be picked at any time but are best when flowers begin to bloom. Leaves should be dried and will retain their scent for two to three years. They may be used in potpourri, sachets, wreaths, and arrangements.
MARJORAM *Latin name: Origanum species* *Hardy herbaceous or shrubby perennial*	There are several varieties of marjoram, all aromatic, that grow to a height of 6 inches to 2 feet. They produce white, pink, or purplish flowers and are good to plant throughout the garden.	Marjoram should be planted in well-drained, nutrient-rich, alkaline soil that is somewhat dry. It does well with full sun and midday shade.	Gather leaves at any time and flowers just as they open. Flowers may be hung upside down to air-dry and added to herbal wreaths.
ROSEMARY *Latin name: Rosmarinus officinalis* *Tender evergreen perennial*	Rosemary leaves are long and narrow, dark green above and silver below. The flowers are usually pale blue but can occasionally be pink or white. This highly aromatic herb is available in upright or prostrate varieties.	Rosemary needs excellent drainage. It is more fragrant in limey soil, so eggshells or potash may be added to regular soil. Protect rosemary from cold winds and grow in a sunny spot.	Harvest at any time. Hang to dry and use for herbal wreaths and arrangements. Leaves are excellent for potpourri crafting.
SAGE *Latin name: Salvia officinalis* *Evergreen shrub*	Purple-blue flowers, soft, downy gray foliage, and a strong herbal fragrance are the hallmarks of this wonderful plant.	Full sun, well-drained soil, and moderate watering will produce herbs for the mid-border.	Sage leaves press well. They can also be hung upside down in small bunches to air-dry. It works well in silver wreaths and adds color to green projects.
SWEET ANNIE *Latin name: Artemisia annua* *Annual herb*	Tall, feathery, aromatic plumes of soft green, maturing to golden brown, grow on upright plants. These can reach a height of 3 to 5 feet.	Grow sweet annie in full sun and average, well-drained soil with moderate watering. Plant it toward the back of a bed.	Harvest when fully mature. Hang upside down to air-dry. Its wonderful fragrance and wispy texture make sweet annie perfect for wreaths and arrangements.

THE LANGUAGE OF FLOWERS

or hundreds of years the custom of attributing specific emotions or thoughts to particular flowers has been practiced.

Nosegays of flowers and herbs chosen from a language-of-flowers list carried meanings beyond their beauty. A bouquet of larkspur, sweet basil, and yarrow hung near the door to welcome guests gives the secret message of levity, good wishes, and compassion.

AMARANTH *(globe)*
Unfading love

ANGELICA
Inspiration

ALMOND
Hope

BALM
Sympathy

BACHELOR'S BUTTON
Celibacy

BLUEBELL
Constancy

CARNATION, PINK
Woman's love

CHRYSANTHEMUM, RED
I love

CAMPANULA
Gratitude

DAFFODIL
Regards

DAISY
Innocence

FORGET-ME-NOT
True love

GERANIUM, ROSE OR APPLE-SCENTED
Preference

HIBISCUS
Delicate beauty

HYACINTH, BLUE
Constancy

IVY
Friendship

LEMON BLOSSOMS
Fidelity in love

LILAC, WHITE
Purity, modesty

LILY OF THE VALLEY
Return of happiness

MYRTLE
Love

NARCISSUS
Self-interest

PANSY
Thinking of you

PARSLEY
Festive thoughts

PEACH BLOSSOM
Unequaled charm

PEAR BLOSSOM
Affection

POPPY, RED
Consolation

ROSE
Love

ROSEBUD, RED
Young love

ROSEMARY
Remembrance

SAGE
Virtues of the home

SALVIA, BLUE
You are wise

SUNFLOWER
Above it all

SWEET BASIL
Good wishes

TULIP, RED
Declaration of love

TULIP, YELLOW
Hopeless love

VERONICA
Fidelity

VIOLET, BLUE
Faithfulness

VIOLET, WHITE
Innocence

WATER LILY
Purity of heart

YARROW
Solace

ZINNIA
Thoughts of old friends

PLANNING THE GARDEN

Whether you are beginning with graph paper and seed catalogs, planning an intricate garden, or simply adding a few new plants along the walkway, it is always exciting to think of a garden in terms of the whole.

As with a painting or a banquet, the completed picture will always be more harmonious if thought is given to color and form.

Iris leaves add elegant straight lines long after blooms have faded. Sunflowers create a cheerful golden backdrop when building a fence is too much bother. Field poppies will often grow up through baby's breath and forget-me-nots to bring a splash of color near a stone bench.

Plan the garden to fit your lifestyle. Consider the time available for tending and weeding. Plant small garden areas to view from windows. Herbs planted near the kitchen door will be convenient for both cooking and crafting.

The plans given are intended as guidelines to be adapted to your own space. A patio garden of crafter-friendly plants will suit townhouses and small city courtyards. Plant groupings can be used for additions to existing beds or planted as island gardens in a lawn area. The color garden plan offers areas for blocks of color.

Making a garden of your own is an exciting way to get to know plants better and understand the garden's needs. Catalogs of seeds and plants are most helpful in creating a plan. The Resource Guide on page 162 lists excellent seed and plant sources. Read plant descriptions with attention to height, blooming time, water, soil, and light requirements.

Climate-zone charts are usually provided. Consider leaf size and color, plant shape, and habits. Silver-leafed plants add contrast to otherwise green areas. Tall plants create focal points and can be planted to screen a view behind the garden or to ensure privacy. Where space allows, try placing several plants of the same variety together to increase their visual effect. Be sure to allow for growing room. A rule of thumb is 1 square foot per plant, or 9 plants per square yard, which should allow sufficient growing space. Most perennials can be divided in the fall if they become overgrown. Position annuals where they will not disturb the perennials' root system when planted or removed.

The shape of a garden will be determined largely by the area to be cultivated. Pathways will need to be wide enough to accommodate a wheelbarrow if one is used. The width of planted areas should allow for weeding toward the back of beds. Plan gentle curves to please the eye and add a bench for moments of peaceful reflection. Statuary, bee skeps, and bird baths all add a focal point and a personal touch to the design.

Making the Plan

MATERIALS:

Plant list

Graph paper

Pad of tracing paper

Pen or pencil

Masking tape

Ruler

Tape measure

STEP 1

Use measuring tape to measure outdoor area to be planted. Determine how many squares on graph paper will be needed to represent 1 square foot— e.g., four squares horizontally and vertically will be 1 square foot. What is important is that the same number of squares be used in each direction. Allow space for writing plant names.

STEP 2

Tape one sheet of tracing paper over graph paper. Draw the shape of your garden consistent with the scale determined in Step 1. Changing the planting arrangement is part of the planning process, so do not hesitate to discard the tracing paper and start fresh.

STEP 3

Consult plant lists and draw circles or shapes to represent individual plants or groupings. Place tall plants toward the back. Plants of medium height should be midway, and low-growing plants should be placed toward the front. Write the name and variety of plant within the shape where it is to be planted.

The Patio Garden

Easily grown and close at hand is the key to a pretty garden area that doubles as an outdoor room and furnishes materials for crafting all summer. Substitute your favorite plants and adjust this garden to suit your own space. Experiment with plants grouped for leaf color as well as color of flowers. Garden centers often have a gardening information desk to help with questions about plants. Good garden shops can usually order hard-to-find plants, or you may choose to use one of the excellent plant and seed suppliers listed in the Resource Guide on page 162.

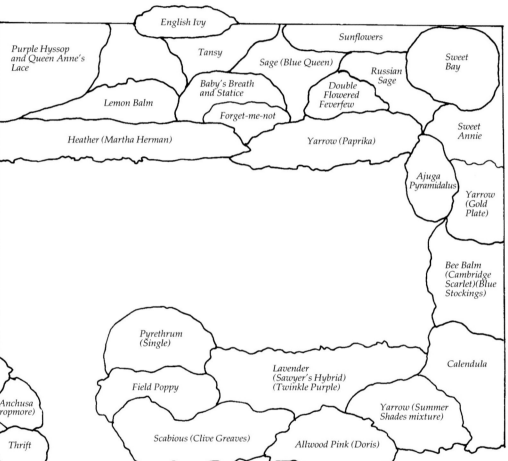

English Ivy

Purple Hyssop and Queen Anne's Lace

Tansy

Sunflowers

Sage (Blue Queen)

Sweet Bay

Russian Sage

Baby's Breath and Statice

Double Flowered Feverfew

Lemon Balm

Forget-me-not

Sweet Annie

Heather (Martha Herman)

Yarrow (Paprika)

Ajuga Pyramidalus

Yarrow (Gold Plate)

Bee Balm (Cambridge Scarlet)(Blue Stockings)

Pyrethrum (Single)

Lavender (Sawyer's Hybrid) (Twinkle Purple)

Calendula

Field Poppy

Rose

Anchusa (Dropmore)

Larkspur

Stock

Thrift

Yarrow (Moonshine)

Thyme (Silver Posie)

Scabious (Clive Greaves)

Allwood Pink (Doris)

Yarrow (Summer Shades mixture)

Container Gardening

There is never enough room for the garden of our dreams. When physical space is limited or there is little time to tend beds, plants in containers will do beautifully. Be sure to add drainage holes to unconventional containers such as tin pitchers and old watering cans. Plants in flower may be brought indoors for occasional display.

Plants and Bulbs for Container Gardening

Calendula

Chrysanthemum

Daffodil

Forget-me-not

Lemon verbena

Lobelia

Miniature rose

Pink

Scented-leaf geranium

Tulip

Small varieties of yarrow

Herbs for Container Gardening

Basil

Catmint

Feverfew

Lemon balm

Oregano

Rosemary

Sage

Santolina

Sweet marjoram

Thyme

Containers

Clay pots

Clay strawberry jars

Painted metal watering cans

Plastic-lined baskets

Stone urns

Tinware

Window boxes

Wooden barrels

Unused wheelbarrows

Plant large tubs with pineapple sage, bay, lavender, and delphiniums. Tubs can be moved to sheds or a garage for overwintering.

THE CRAFTER'S COLOR GARDEN

Create a peaceful garden of color and a retreat from a busy life at the same time. Place a little garden bench at the end of a walkway near the lavender to facilitate bee-watching and thinking positive thoughts.

This garden can be adapted by incorporating a section of this plan into your garden or choosing a color scheme to plant along a walkway.

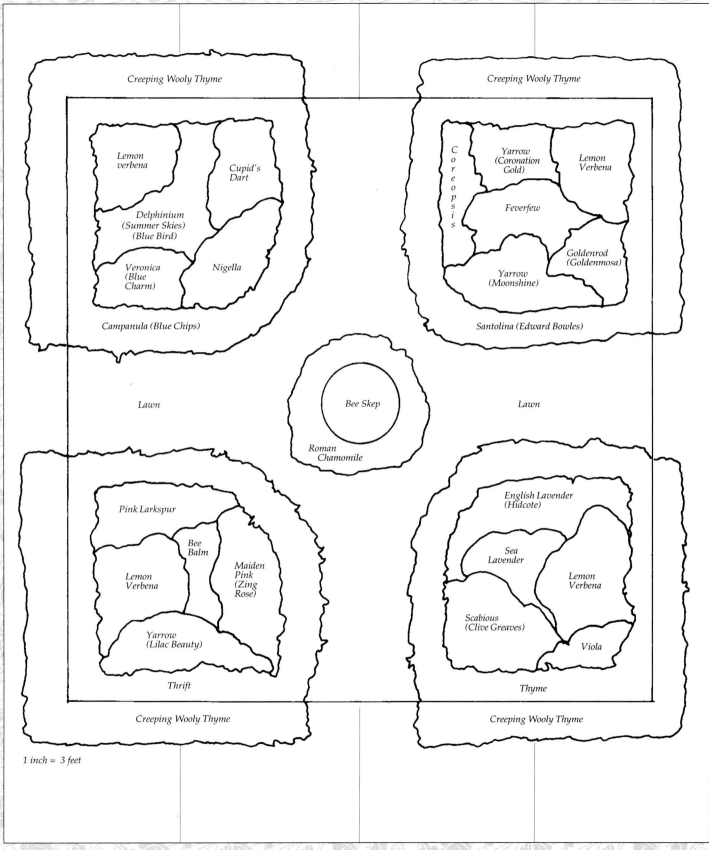

Creeping Wooly Thyme

Lemon
verbena

Cupid's
Dart

Delphinium
(Summer Skies)
(Blue Bird)

Veronica
(Blue
Charm)

Nigella

Campanula (Blue Chips)

Creeping Wooly Thyme

Coreopsis

Yarrow
(Coronation
Gold)

Lemon
Verbena

Feverfew

Goldenrod
(Goldenmosa)

Yarrow
(Moonshine)

Santolina (Edward Bowles)

Lawn

Bee Skep

Roman
Chamomile

Lawn

Pink Larkspur

Bee
Balm

Lemon
Verbena

Maiden
Pink
(Zing
Rose)

Yarrow
(Lilac Beauty)

Thrift

English Lavender
(Hidcote)

Sea
Lavender

Lemon
Verbena

Scabious
(Clive Greaves)

Viola

Thyme

Creeping Wooly Thyme

Creeping Wooly Thyme

1 inch = 3 feet

27

DRYING AND PRESERVING FLOWERS

Saving the blooms of summer for crafting use requires very little time and equipment. A display of colorful bunches of herbs and blossoms hung to dry is a beautiful addition to the home and provides materials to use throughout the crafting year.

ir-drying and desiccant-drying are easy methods to master. Preserving plant material with glycerin requires more experimentation and gives a soft, leathery feeling to botanicals.

The method to choose depends upon the look you are seeking for the project. Air-drying results in slightly shriveled leaves and flowers. Some flowers tend to retain their color well, whereas others fade very quickly. Desiccant-dried flowers keep their form and color well, while glycerin preservation is recommended for foliage and berries.

Air-Drying

The condition of the air surrounding the materials being dried determines the speed of drying. Warm, dry air quickens this process. Low light will help maintain the color of dried materials.

Collect botanicals for drying after dew has evaporated but before midday. Small bunches are better to hang than larger ones because flowers, once dried, are fragile and may break if they become tangled. It is best to wait until roses are open before drying in order to have a fuller shape. Use garden twine or ribbon scraps to tie stems together.

The time required for drying depends on both the atmosphere and the plants being dried. Generally roses will dry in two weeks, while larkspur may be ready in one week. Remove bunches when dried and store in an airtight container until they are to be used.

To Make a Drying Rack

Hanging racks for home-drying flowers can be made from old wooden window frames. Remove glass panes, paint the frame in your favorite color, and add a screw eye to each corner for hanging. Thread pieces of picture wire through each eye and twist the ends together tightly. Attach hooks to the ceiling for hanging the rack.

Desiccant Drying

Silica gel is the most reliable desiccant-drying method because it allows the blooms to retain their shape and color and gives them a chance to dry at a slow, even pace. The silica granules are quite light and will not damage delicate petals. Each manufacturer encloses instructions that should be followed carefully. The method is simple. Plastic, tin, or glass containers with airtight lids are perfect. Place flowers and leaves, evenly spaced, facing upward on a light layer of silica gel. Gently sprinkle with the silica granules until the plants are well covered. Drying flowers can be layered if containers are deep enough. Some flowers and herbs dry within six or seven days; others take longer. Experiment with times, and if you will be drying materials all summer, it is a good idea to keep notes.

Freeze-Drying

Freeze-drying, acknowledged as one of the finest methods of food preservation, has recently been adapted to flowers. This commercial process allows for maximum retention of floral shape and color. Special machines freeze the blooms at a temperature of -30 degrees Fahrenheit for at least seven days.

Freeze-dried flowers, though delicate, are easy to work with and ship well when packed carefully. These flowers can even be tinted with color or accented with a wash of metallic acrylic paint.

Preserving with Floral Dips

After flowers have been dried by one of the methods listed, floral dips may be used. They will preserve the color of the flower as dried and add flexibility. Each manufacturer of chemical floral dips provides detailed instructions on the use of its product that should be followed carefully. It is essential to work in a well-ventilated area and protect your skin during this process.

Preserving Flowers with Wax

Small flowers and leaves, as well as some larger specimens, can be preserved by dipping silica-dried blooms into melted wax. This method does not work well with multipetaled flowers such as roses, as petals tend to stick together when waxed. Miniature roses and rosebuds, however, are excellent candidates for waxing.

The wax used to treat flowers can be either a melted white candle or candle-making wax. Scented votive candles will melt down easily and cover material with a perfumed coating. Pure beeswax will give flowers and leaves an antiqued look and release the sweet scent of honey in the air. Flowers will require stems to hold on to when dipping. If stems are short, use florist's wire and florist's tape to add length (see page 35).

Waxed floral arrangements have a lovely, soft texture and will retain color and shape very well. Always display waxed flowers away from heat sources and preferably out of direct sunlight. Avoid placing lit candles near waxed flowers as wax is a highly flammable material.

MATERIALS:

Selection of silica-dried flowers and leaves with 6-8-inch stems

Double boiler with a top pan large enough to accommodate the depth of the flower heads to be dipped

Enough melted wax to completely cover flower heads

1 block florist's foam

Waxed paper

STEP 1

Melt wax in top pan of double boiler. If dipping tulips, depth of wax should be approximately 3 to 5 inches. If dipping daisies, depth of wax should be approximately 2 to 3 inches. If candles are melted, remove wicks from melted wax.

STEP 2

Place florist's foam on center of waxed paper. Hold flower by stem and dip flower head into wax. Remove at once. Place stem in foam block. Allow wax coating to set completely, approximately 10 minutes, before arranging flowers.

Drying Fruit

Dried fruit adds colorful natural shapes to projects. This fruit is available through craft-supply stores, florists, and some natural-materials mail-order companies. Some fruit can be successfully dried at home. Always dry far more material than needed to assure enough perfect specimens for projects.

Drying Citrus

Oranges, lemons, and limes sliced with a sharp knife to a thickness of ¼ to ½-inch can be slow-dried in the oven. Place waxed paper or a thin layer of silica gel on cookie sheets, arrange slices so they do not touch one another, and place in a warm oven (about 200 degrees) with the oven door slightly open. Six to 10 hours of slow heating will be enough time for slices to dry. Turn slices a few times to allow even moisture evaporation. Granules of silica gel may be brushed off dried fruit with a soft brush or left on to create a sugar-coated effect.

Drying Apples

Apples dry well using the oven method. Waxed paper, oven temperature, and time are the same as for drying citrus. Again, keep the oven door slightly ajar.

Prepare apples by washing and coring them. Cut slices ¼ inch thick. Centers can be recut with small star aspic cutters for a pretty center shape. Red delicious apples work well and retain their bright-red-peel color. Dip slices in a bowl filled with a mixture of ½ water and ½ lemon juice. Commercial canning products to prevent discoloration work equally well.

Drying Pomegranates

Pomegranates air-dry beautifully. Simply place fruit in a warm place, away from direct sunlight until they are dry. This usually takes from two to three months, but the fruit can be displayed while drying.

Glycerin Preservation

Mix one part glycerin with two parts of hot water. Stir until thoroughly mixed. This volume will yield enough to preserve a vaseful of foliage. Extra solution will be required as stems absorb the liquid. Always choose perfect leaves for glycerin preservation as natural flaws will be magnified by this process.

Cut small branches of leaves. Trim off any damaged leaves. Cut deep crisscross slits in stem ends. Scrape away 2 to 3 inches of bark from stem ends to allow for added absorption of glycerin solution. Place prepared stems in a vase of solution. Leaves will generally darken to shades of brown and acquire a glossy look.

Time required for preserving will be from one to three weeks, depending on the size of branch and the type of leaf. Keep glycerin solution topped up until botanicals have absorbed enough liquid to produce glossy leaves that look slightly waxy.

SUGGESTED BOTANICALS FOR GLYCERIN PRESERVATION

Bay, Berries, Camellia leaves, Eucalyptus, Holly, Ivy, Maple, Maidenhair fern, Rose briars, Pine and Cedar boughs

BOWS

Bouquets and wreaths tied in ribbons of silk are a lovely decorative accent. Beautiful, no-sew ruffled and gathered ribbon bows can be made easily using wired ribbon.

This is a very simple procedure, and the results are often breathtaking. It requires nothing more than pushing the ribbon back on the wire after having secured one end. The difference between a ruffled and a gathered ribbon has to do with whether one or both edges have been pushed back: pushing back one edge of the ribbon will create a ruffle; pushing both edges back results in a gathered ribbon. Gathered ribbons may be used for the center section around a ruffled bow. These bows hold their shape especially well and have a rich, full look. A good rule of thumb is to double the amount of ribbon required for a normal bow.

Ruffled Bow

1 yard of 1½-inch-wide wired ribbon

Glue gun/glue sticks

These materials will form a single bow, 4 inches wide overall, with 4-inch streamers.

STEP 1

Cut a 10-inch piece of ribbon from ribbon length and set aside. Fold one end of remaining ribbon over ¼ inch onto itself. Press to secure.

STEP 2

Gently work one wire of opposite end out of ribbon. Hold wire firmly and gently push ribbon back along wire. This will create a ruffle. Continue until the entire length of ribbon is ruffled. Fold extended wire over onto itself at end of ruffle. Secure with a dot of hot glue. Do not cut extended wire.

STEP 3

Form a two-loop bow with gathered edge toward center of loops (see page 34). Use extended wire to wind around bow center and secure. Secure wire end with a dot of hot glue.

STEP 4

Use remaining ribbon piece to tie around wired section at bow center. This will create both a bow center and streamers.

Gathered Bow

Follow instructions for making a ruffled bow with one change: Push ribbon back on both wires instead of just one wire. A length of gathered or ungathered ribbon may be tied around wired center section to create streamers. If a gathered piece is used for the streamer/center section, double the length of ribbon required for this piece.

Forming the Bow

MATERIALS:

1 piece of ribbon for bow portion

1 piece of ribbon for streamers

One 4-inch piece florist's wire

Wire cutter

STEP 1

Hold one end of ribbon cut for bow between thumb and index finger. Form a loop of desired fullness.

STEP 2

Hold bow center, twist ribbon, and form a second loop opposite the first. Secure center with a twist of wire. Use wire cutter to trim wire ends.

STEP 3

Tie remaining ribbon length around bow center. Trim bow streamer to desired length and shape.

Double-Fuller Bow

Double ribbon length required if forming a double bow; triple length for a six-loop bow. Follow the steps for forming a single bow. After second loop has been formed, twist ribbon again to form a loop on top of first loop. Twist and loop ribbon from side to side until a bow of desired fullness has been formed.

FLORAL CRAFTER'S TOOLS

The last bouquet of the year is often one of this and one of that. A lone pink zinnia, a single stem of tansy, one red rose...the time has come to put the garden to bed and wait for the seed catalogs to arrive in January.

Floral Picks

For use with foam or straw-based wreath forms.

Short wooden picks with a tapered, sharpened point and a piece of wire attached to the opposite end.

Small sprigs of herbs or single stems are placed alongside the wooden pick and secured with a twist of wire. The wooden point is then inserted into the base of the project.

Florist's Pins

Hairpin shapes of florist's wire—they are used to secure mosses and herbs to straw and foam shapes.

Florist's Tape

A thin, stretchy, slightly tacky adhesive tape. Wrap stems or small nosegay sprigs together by stretching and rolling stems together in tape. Pressing lightly will activate adhesive.

Florist's tape is available in greens, brown, and white to match the materials being taped.

Florist's Wire

Precut wire lengths of green sold in several gauges or thicknesses. Used to lengthen stems, it is usually attached with floral tape.

Glue Gun

Invaluable electric tool that heats glue and releases it when trigger mechanism is pulled. Glue guns are available for low-temperature glue and hot glue melts.

Glue Sticks

Available in low and high temperatures. Always check the glue gun manufacturers's requirements.

Spool Wires

Florist's wire is also available in a continuous piece on a spool. This wire is perfect for making wreaths and garlands as it can be wound around materials to secure.

Wire Cutter

Tool made expressly for cutting through all gauges of wire. Cutting wire with scissors will soon ruin the blade.

Tip For Forming Wreath Bases

Plant materials can be used singly to form wreath bases or in combination. Simply form bunches of mixed herbs for wiring or gluing.

WREATHS AND GARLANDS

Botanicals listed in the Materials list for projects should be regarded as guidelines, and therefore substitutions are encouraged. Adapt projects by using flowers, leaves, and herbs of your choice.

esigning wreaths is one of the most exciting aspects of crafting from the garden. Simple herbal wreaths, full of texture and aroma, are signs of welcome on the kitchen door. Elaborate wreaths of fruit and flowers, created to coordinate with the color scheme of a room, are the crowning glory of decorating. No matter how many wreaths you craft, there is always inspiration for another. The wreaths presented in this book have been crafted of flowers, herbs, leaves, and fruit—all natural and dried or used fresh and allowed to dry in place. Silk flowers can be substituted in any project and also produce a beautiful effect. They will not fade or lose their shape.

Readymade wreath bases of straw, grapevine, twigs, moss, and plastic foam are available in crafts shops and florist's supply shops. Each type of base is useful, so choose the one that best suits the wreath you are designing. A listing of wreath bases follows, and a glossary of tools commonly used in creating wreaths and garlands can be found on page 35.

Most of the wreaths pictured in this book were assembled on straw bases with the use of a glue gun. Hot glue holds materials securely, and the process is faster than individual wiring of materials.

Creating wreath bases from herbs gathered is especially rewarding and an excellent way to make use of the summer harvest. Often a single plant of sweet annie or silver artemisia produces enough material to make several wreaths. Herbs can be added to straw wreaths at harvesttime for later use.

The methods of wreath assembly are simple, and their use depends upon the wreath design. Try these simple base constructions using purchased mosses or greens from the garden.

HERBS AND GREENS SUITABLE FOR A WREATH BASE

Boxwood, Cedar boughs, Eucalyptus, Feverfew, Heather, Holly, Lamb's ear, Marjoram, Oregano, Pine boughs, Sage, Santolina, Silver king artemisia, Statice, Sweet annie

Assemble the Wreath Base

METHOD 1— THE WIRED WREATH BASE

MATERIALS:

One 10-inch-diameter wire wreath form

1 spool florist's wire

Large bunch herbs or greens

Wire cutter

STEP 1

Trim all greens or herbs to stems of approximately 6 inches. Place a bunch of 15 to 20 stems together on top of wreath form. Wind spooled wire around stems several times to secure. Do not cut wire.

STEP 2

Lay a second bunch of greens or herbs on wire base just below first bunch. Tops of leaves will cover wired section. Wind wire around stems several times. Continue adding bunches and wiring stems to wreath base until entire wreath form has been covered. Use wire cutter to trim excess wire. Tuck wire end beneath leaves.

The final bunch of greens or herbs will have to be tucked beneath the first. Greens and herbs may be used fresh and allowed to dry in place.

METHOD 2— SINGLE WIRE BASE

A delicate base that can be shaped to an oval or a heart, this base is suitable for the addition of delicate flowers only.

MATERIALS:

18 inches medium-gauge florist's wire

Sphagnum moss

Needle nose pliers

Wire cutter

Glue gun/glue sticks

STEP 1

Using pliers, bend both ends of wire to form loops. To form a circle, hook loops together. Close tightly by pressing with pliers.

STEP 2

Using hot glue, work in small sections and attach small amounts of moss around wire.

Continue gluing moss to wire until entire circle has been covered.

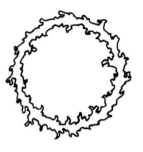

STEP 3 (OPTIONAL)

Bend wreath base to form a heart. Follow the same procedure when gluing an herbal-based wreath. Stems need to be trimmed to a length of 3 to 5 inches.

Assemble the Wreath Base

METHOD 3— PINNED WREATH BASE

Florist's pins are useful for making all moss wreath bases. Herbs and fabrics can also be attached to straw wreath bases with florist's pins.

MATERIALS:

24-30 florist's pins

Moss

One 10-inch-diameter straw wreath base

STEP 1

Using florist's pins, work in small sections and place small handfuls of moss on wreath surface. Push pins through moss and fully into straw wreath to secure. Arrange moss to cover pin loops.

STEP 2

Pin sections of moss around sides of wreath and complete by filling in front section.

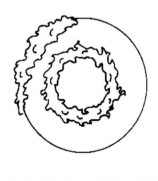

METHOD 4— GLUED WREATH BASE

Large amount of moss or several large bunches dried herbs

10-inch straw wreath base

Glue gun/glue sticks

STEP 1

Use hot glue and work in sections to attach small amounts of moss or dried herbs to sides of wreath. Cover all straw areas.

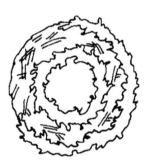

STEP 2

Complete wreath base by filling in top area with moss or botanicals.

Wreaths of Miniature Bouquets

Use floral picks and florist's tape to create miniature bouquets of mixed flowers to make wreaths of mixed botanicals. This method works well for small sprigs of materials and is an excellent way to use leftover botanicals.

MATERIALS:

One 12-inch-diameter straw wreath base

35-40 floral picks

Large selection of small flowers

Sprigs of baby's breath, caspia, and statice

1 roll green florist's tape

Scissors

STEP 1

Place stems of a small mixed bouquet alongside the blunt end of a floral pick. Wind wire around stems to secure.

STEP 2

Using florist's tape, begin wrapping stems, pressing tape gently into place. Leave sharp end of pick exposed. Make all bouquets before proceeding.

STEP 3

Press picks into wreath base. Begin with interior sides of base, followed by outer sides. Complete by filling in center of wreath.

Scent your wreaths by adding essential oils to straw wreath base before assembling. Freshen scent by adding a few drops of essential oil to wreath occasionally.

Garlands

Garlands of dried flowers and herbs can be tailored to decorate any room. Easily fashioned of wire and botanicals, they can be shaped to cornice a window or encircle the posts of your bed. A simple garland glued to an oval mirror frame makes a lovely addition to the entry hall or powder room. Large garlands for the mantel or doorway can include dried fruit, large seedpods, and ornaments. Measure the area to be covered and trim wire to the length of your project. Experiment with herbs and greens collected from the garden. Garlands can be made of combination or single plants.

The width of your garland will be determined by the amount of materials wired together. If an especially large garland is desired, it is best to make two or three garland bases and wind them around one another for added strength before decorating.

Suggested plant material is the same as botanicals for wreath bases (see page 37).

Herbal Garlands

MATERIALS:

Dried or fresh plant material

Heavy-gauge wire

Florist's wire (on spool or individual pieces)

Florist's tape

Wire cutter

Glue gun/glue sticks

STEP 1

Use wire cutter to trim thicker wire to desired length. Place stems of a small bouquet of plant material along wire, allowing wire end to extend about 3 inches into bouquet. Wrap stems several times with florist's wire.

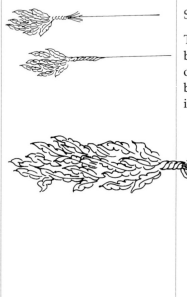

STEP 2

Wind florist's tape around wired stems, pressing gently to secure in place. Trim tape.

STEP 3

Place a second bouquet on top of the first to cover taped section. Wire and tape stems. Continue adding bouquets until the center of wire is reached. Begin at opposite wire end and add bouquets until the center is reached. See illustration below.

STEP 4

The center section may be decorated with a bow or with small sprigs of bouquet material secured in place with hot glue.

Moss Garlands

Garlands of delicate flowers and leaves can be glued on a mossed wire for a delicate and pliable garland. Scent moss with essential oil for added fragrance.

MATERIALS:

Selection of small dried or pressed flowers

Sphagnum moss

Spool of florist's wire

Wire cutter

Glue gun/glue sticks

STEP 1

Using hot glue, work in small sections and glue small amounts of florist's wire to moss. Continue until entire wire has been mossed.

STEP 2

Glue small flowers and leaves to moss and bend garland to desired shape.

All that in this delightful garden grows,
Should happy be, and have
immortal bliss.
—EDMUND SPENCER
1552–1599

NOSEGAYS

Small bouquets of summer flowers tied in bright ribbons and surrounded by a ruff of paper lace are perfect gifts for visitors to the garden.

Nosegays of roses and baby's breath are traditional for wedding parties. Fresh herbs, dried peonies, and autumn leaves are all suitable for making a nosegay. The term "tussie-mussie" was a popular description of small posies given as tokens of affection in Victorian times. These nosegays were often designed to carry a secret message by selecting flowers from the Language of Flowers list (see page 21).

Making a Fresh Nosegay

Choose fresh, healthy material from the garden, placing stems in water so flowers and foliage have a good drink before proceeding.

MATERIALS:

Paper-lace nosegay holder

1 rose, central flower, or grouping of similar flowers

Selection of smaller flowers, herbal sprigs, and leaves

Baby's breath or airy filler flowers

1 yard ribbon

Florist's tape

Scissors or garden clippers

STEP 1

Wind florist's tape around central flower(s) stem(s).

STEP 2

Gradually add smaller flowers, leaves, and herbs around central flower or group. Tape stems to main wrapped stem.

STEP 3

Place taped stem through hole in center of nosegay holder. Push holder up on stem until paper lace surrounds nosegay. Tie a double bow around stem just below paper holder. Store fresh nosegays in refrigerator with stem placed in a small glass of water until presented.

Dried-Flower Nosegays

Nosegays of dried materials have the advantages of becoming a keepsake and incorporating scented oils. Hot glue may be used to construct dried-flower posies. Bows may be glued on top of paper ruff, and charms or a gift tag may be added. Selected fresh materials, such as lamb's ear leaves and strawflowers, may be assembled in the fresh state and allowed to air-dry. Essential oil may be added by drops to mosses and leaves to perfume dried-flower nosegays.

POTPOURRI

Collecting petals and leaves for potpourri can be done during the entire garden season. Flowers cut for the home and enjoyed as bouquets offer petals and greens. Rose petals and lavender, yarrow and strawflowers—there are supplies at hand from spring until winter.

T hough harvesting is an ongoing process, putting the garden to bed in the autumn seems the perfect time to think of scenting winter rooms and adding natural colors to the home.

Dried petals, pods, and leaves have reached sufficient numbers by autumn to create large quantities of potpourri. Seasoning the scents usually takes a few weeks, so sachets and other scented projects can be timed perfectly for Christmas giving.

Gather all materials after dew has evaporated from flowers and leaves but well before the midday sun has faded petals. Old, large window screens, stacked with wood strips for spacing, are good for air-drying petals in quantity. A warm, low-light area is best for drying petals.

Place even layers of petals on screens to dry. Thick mats of petals will result in slower drying and often moldy petals.

Plan your potpourri for color as well as scent. Dry a few whole flowers to decorate the top of potpourri placed in bowls, baskets, or gift boxes.

Dried botanicals are blended with a fixative, such as powdered orrisroot and small amounts of essential or pure oils. Potpourri can also be prepared in a moist form. The moist form offers especially rich scent and lasts for a long time.

Though dry potpourris are blended after many petals have been collected, moist potpourri begins with the first roses of summer. To create moist potpourri, a large quantity of fragrant roses is needed.

Making Potpourri

Measure dry botanicals listed in a recipe, or create blends using quantities listed in a recipe as your guideline. The amount of oils required can be increased or diminished depending on the amount of potpourri you are making. Fixatives should also be adjusted to the amount of oils used. Plastics and metals are not recommended for potpourri crafting. Keep wooden spoons used with essential oils separate from kitchen spoons.

MATERIALS:

Potpourri recipe

Botanicals

Essential oils

Fixative

Large crockery bowl

Wooden spoon

Glass eyedropper

Crockery cup or small bowl

Paper bag

Clothespins

STEP 1

Place all dried materials in a large bowl. Gently blend with hands or wooden spoon. Be sure not to break delicate petals.

STEP 2

Place fixative in a cup or small bowl. Add essential oil(s) using eyedropper. Mix oils with fixative until saturated.

STEP 3

Add scented fixative to botanicals. Mix gently.

STEP 4

Place potpourri in paper bag, folding top over to close. Secure with clothespins and store away from direct sunlight for four to six weeks.

Tip For Storing Potpourri

Garlic jars are perfect for storing moist potpourri, as their openwork allows scent to escape while potpourri is kept slightly damp.

Dry Potpourri

Mixtures of dried botanicals have been used to scent the house and heal the soul for centuries. The art of making these potpourri mixtures is as simple as saving petals from the garden and blending them with scented oils and a fixative, which holds the scent. The basic procedure for making potpourri is only a guideline, so experiment with blends of essential oils and adapt recipes according to the materials you have on hand.

Bulk botanicals, essential oils, and fixatives are available through some crafts stores, health-food shops, and the suppliers listed in the Resource Guide on page 162. Scent can determine the feeling of a room. Spicy cinnamon and apple scents create a cozy ambience on a winter's day. Sweet rose and lilac perfume the air with the scent of a spring garden. Mix your potpourri to set the mood you desire. Mixing oils for potpourri entails choosing a base, or underlying scent, into which lesser amounts — perhaps just a drop or two — of complementary oils are added. Scents fall into several different categories: floral, herbal, citrus, spice, woodsy, and exotic.

Potpourri colors can be tailored to suit the decor of a room. Sunflower petals mixed with deep-red rose petals and sage leaves will carry the colors of a favorite chair to another part of the room. Delicate pink and white petals in a small glass bowl add a sweet touch of color to the nursery.

Even the smallest garden will provide botanicals to dry for potpourri. Try blending petals of a single color range for a dramatic potpourri. Potpourris can be placed in the blender if hard materials such as nutmegs, twigs, and cinnamon sticks are removed. The ground particles are useful for covering plastic foam balls with potpourri. Fill a large bowl with potpourri balls of individual colors for a spectacular centerpiece. The plastic foam ball is simply covered with white craft glue and rolled in the ground potpourri.

Moist Rose Potpourri

MATERIALS:

50-80 fragrant roses, collected over several weeks

2 cups coarse, non-iodized salt

Large crock

Circle of plastic cut to fit inside of crock

Heavy stone that fits inside crock

STEP 1

Remove petals from roses. Dry to a slightly leathery stage. Place a layer of rose petals approximately 1 inch deep in crock. Sprinkle approximately ½ cup of salt on petals. Add a second layer of petals and salt. Continue layering petals and salt until all petals are used. Place plastic piece over last layer and weigh down with stone. When more material is gathered, continue adding layers of leathery petals and salt until the crock is full.

STEP 2

Occasionally drain the expressed rose liquid from the crock. The first draining will produce a clear pink, rose-scented liquid that can be used in the bath or as a hand rinse. Later drainings are useful for crafting but will be slightly cloudy.

STEP 3

After 10 to 12 months, moist potpourri will be crumbly and sweetly rose-scented. Remove from crock, draining any liquid. Store in covered baskets or ginger jars with pierced lids to release the rose scent slowly. This scent lasts for years and can be used as a base for additional petals and essential oils.

Mixed-Flower Moist Potpourri

MATERIALS:

5 cups moist rose potpourri

2 cups dried lavender

1 cup dried lemon verbena

4 tablespoons orrisroot powder

10 drops essential rose oil

STEP 1

Prepare Moist Rose Potpourri (see recipe, above). When crumbly, blend with lavender and lemon verbena in a large crockery bowl. Mix rose oil with orrisroot and add to flowers.

STEP 2

Place mixture in a paper bag and seal. Allow to cure for six weeks.

Fixatives

Although potpourri can be made without a fixative, the duration of its scent is short-lived. A fixative absorbs the oil mixture and helps retain the volatile scented oils.

Iris germanica tubers, gathered when plants are about three years old, are dried and ground to create orrisroot. Oakmoss, cellulose, and gum benzoin are also commonly used fixatives.

Tip For Sensitive Crafters

People with known allergies should check with their physician before handling potpourri ingredients. Occasionally essential oils and natural fixatives cause respiratory or topical reactions.

Essential Oils

Essential oils are the second key ingredient in potpourri blends. These can be purchased in a pure botanical form or in commercial blends. Use a small non-metal cup or bowl for blending oils. Add oils drop by drop until the scent pleases you. Since you may want to re-create a particular blend, it is advisable to record your experiments. Oils from all categories can be blended successfully.

Begin with a base scent into which single drops of other oils are added.

FLORAL

Damask rose, French rose, Honeysuckle, Jasmine, Lavender, Lilac, Lily of the valley, Parma violet, Tuberose

HERBAL

Basil, Chamomile, Pennyroyal, Peppermint, Rosemary, Sage, Thyme

CITRUS

Bitter orange, Lemon, Lemon balm, Lemon grass, Lemon verbena, Lime, Sweet orange, Tangerine

SPICY

Allspice, Bitter almond, Cinnamon, Cloves, Vanilla

WOODSY

Balsam, Cedar, Cypress, Juniper, Rosewood, Sandalwood, White pine

EXOTIC

Amber, Frankincense, Myrrh, Patchouli, Ylang-ylang

Botanicals for Potpourri Color

RED

Carnation, Chili peppers, Geranium, Heather, Holly berries, Pineapple sage, Rose, Rosehip

PINK

Carnation, Geranium, Globe amaranth, Heather, Larkspur, Rose, Statice, Strawflower

WHITE/CREAM

Alyssum, Aster, Carnation, Daisy, Globe amaranth, Jasmine, Larkspur, Lavender leaves, Rose, Sage, Statice, Stock, Strawflower

YELLOW, GOLD, ORANGE

Calendula, Chamomile, Citrus peel, Marigold, Orange slices, Rose, Sunflower, Zinnia

GREEN

Balsam tips, Bay leaves, Ivy, Lemon balm, Lemon verbena, Mint, Moss, Oregano, Pine needles, Rose leaves, Rosemary

BLUE

Aster, Bachelor's buttons (cornflower), Borage, Delphinium, Forget-me-not

PURPLE

Aster, Delphinium, Heather, Larkspur, Lavender, Lilac, Rose, Statice, Stock, Thyme, Violet

EARTH TONES

Allspice, Cedar shavings, Cinnamon sticks, Cloves, Eucalyptus pods, Juniper berries, Nutmeg, Small pinecones

PRESSING HERBS & FLOWERS

Small flowers of every kind press well and are useful for application to many projects. Handmade cards and gift tags become even more personal with pressed flowers from the summer garden. Boxes and decorative plates can be embellished with pressed botanicals.

Collect flowers when the dew has evaporated and place them in a flower press or an unused telephone directory immediately after picking.

A simple flower press can be assembled for small quantities of pressed materials. This type of press is made of two beveled wooden plaques found at most crafts stores. Thin leather cords instead of screws fasten it. Paint the press exterior or decoupage pressed flowers on the front and varnish. The press shown has painted borders and a square of French provincial wrapping paper glued on. Cover surfaces have been protected with matte acrylic varnish. Presses of all sizes are available with bolt and screw fasteners.

These, too, can be painted and decorated.

To use a flower press, place a few sheets of newspaper, cut to fit the press, on the press base. Add one piece of absorbent paper, such as blotting paper, smooth-textured paper towels, or artist's newsprint. Position flowers, leaves, and herbs on this paper. Botanicals should not touch one another. Place a second sheet of absorbent paper on top of botanicals, followed by more newspaper. Continue to layer in this manner—newspaper, absorbent paper, botanicals, absorbent paper—until all botanicals have been used. Usually 10 layers are sufficient to dry a good quantity of material. Label the press or top sheet with the date of pressing and place press in a dry, warm place.

Six to eight weeks will ensure complete drying for most plants. Delicate botanicals will dry faster, however.

You can use white craft glue, acrylic medium, or acrylic varnish to secure pressed flowers to paper, wood, and wooden surfaces. Acrylic medium is used to affix pressed flowers to glass surfaces. A thin coat of acrylic medium or varnish may be brushed over flowers for protection.

Flowers glued to papers can also be sealed with a thin coat of melted wax. Try a scented wax to perfume flowers.

Tip For Storing Pressed Flowers

An excellent way to store pressed flowers is in clear plastic protector sheets often used for slides. Place a single flower in each slide pocket and store in a ring binder for easy access.

TOPIARIES

Ivy and ferns, growing in the cool shade beneath the spreading branches of an old tree, offer the most soothing of garden tapestries, green on green. Shapes are defined by the most subtle color variations. Green is also the color of healing, so a break in the garden is in order to calm frazzled nerves.

Growing topiaries requires a little patience and pruning practice, but the results are well worth the effort. Select strong, young plants for topiary training. Ivy plants will give a head start, as their tendrils can be wound around wire shapes for an instant effect.

2 small ivy plants

6-inch-diameter clay pot

Potting-soil mix

Garden twine

Coil of heavy-gauge wire

Pebbles or shards of broken clay pots

Wire cutter

Needle nose pliers

STEP 1

Uncoil and cut a length of wire long enough to accommodate desired topiary size. A good rule for measurement is 3 to 3 ½ times longer than the height of the completed topiary. Using pliers, twist wire ends together to form a stake long enough to reach the bottom of the clay pot.

STEP 2

Using pliers or your hands, shape wire loop.

STEP 3

Place pebbles or shards at the bottom of the clay pot. Fill pot halfway with potting soil. Place both plants in the center of the pot, their shoots facing in opposite directions.

Place additional soil around plants. Be sure to match soil level of previous pot. Tap pot on table surface to settle roots. Water well, but allow excess water to drain.

STEP 4

Place topiary-form stake in pot between plants. Push firmly into place. Gently wrap shoots around exposed stake and form. Tie in place with small pieces of garden twine.

As your plant becomes stronger, the ties can be removed to allow healthy growth.

Plant woody stemmed plants such as boxwood and rosemary in the same manner, trimming leaves and shoots from the area growing along topiary stake.

Topiary Care

Once your topiary has filled its form, pinch back new shoots to encourage a full shape.

Water your growing topiary when the soil appears to be dry. Follow the growing instructions on the supplier's plant stake found in most pottedplants; or consult a garden encyclopedia.

SUGGESTED PLANTS

Boxwood, Ivy, Lemon verbena, Myrtle, Rosemary, Santolina, Sweet bay, Thyme, Wormwood

Tip For Keeping Flowers Fresh

Mist fresh-flower wreaths often to keep flowers fresh-looking. Store wreaths in refrigerator at night to extend their freshness.

SPRING GARDEN PROJECTS

Roses seem redder, daisies a little brighter, when the violet blooms at their side.
Combine the colors you love in the garden, for in nature they are all perfect together.

FRESH-FLOWER WREATH

ombine all types of herbs and flowers according to the season. Cherries and other small fruit can be wired in among the flowers for a beautiful summer effect. Prepare a wreath of fresh culinary herbs for use in the kitchen; sprigs may be removed for cooking and replaced as needed.

Use a fresh wreath on the table with pillar candles for a romantic centerpiece. If fresh wreaths are prepared the day before a party, place them in the refrigerator at night. To freshen flowers and leaves, spray lightly with water.

MATERIALS: *(substitute any fresh flowers and herbs you like)*

One 10-inch wire wreath form

4 white roses

5 pink roses

6 pink sweet william

9 stems narcissus

15-20 delphiniums

1 block florist's foam suitable for fresh flowers

Sphagnum moss

Liquid plant food for cut flowers (optional)

1 spool light-gauge florist's wire

Wire cutter

Knife

Garden clipper

Pad of newspapers

Prepare flowers by recutting stem ends and placing them in water for an hour to allow blooms to have a long drink.

STEP 1

Fill sink ½ full with cool water. Add liquid or powdered cut-flower food (optional). Soak foam block until it is completely saturated, usually 15 to 20 minutes. Place moss in water until ready to use.

STEP 2

Place a thick pad of newspapers on worktable. Place wire wreath form on top of newspapers. Using knife, cut florist's foam into sections that will fit into your wreath base. Place these into base. Use spool of wire and bend wire end around wreath form. Wind wire around wreath to secure florist's foam in place. Do not cut wire end.

STEP 3

Place wet moss on top surface of foam. Wind wire around wreath to secure moss in place. Using wire cutter, cut wire end and twist around wire form. Tuck in end.

STEP 4

Using garden clipper, cut flower stems at an angle to a length of approximately 2 inches. Arrange them around wreath in a pleasing pattern, pressing stems into moist foam.

BLUE PROVINCIAL BIRDHOUSE

Blue morning glories tumble over the garden wall, the feeder is filled for hungry sparrows, the garden awakens and it is time for a cup of tea on the bench.

Early hours in the garden, spent in reflection, are the best preparation for a busy day.

MATERIALS:

One 9x3x3-inch wooden birdhouse

14x14-inch piece blue provincial-print fabric

7 red miniature rosebuds

10 - 15 spikes dried lavender

Five 9-inch stems sea lavender

3 tall sprigs thyme or oregano

Sphagnum moss

Moss-green and deep rose acrylic paint

Round brush

Sharp scissors

Tracing paper

Pen

Straight pins

Masking tape

Ruler

Spray adhesive

Glue gun/glue sticks

STEP 1

Remove perches from birdhouse. With brush and deep rose paint, paint inside of holes and bird perches. Using moss-green paint and round brush, paint house base and roof. Allow paint to dry before proceeding.

STEP 2

To make a pattern for fabric sides, place one sheet of tracing paper against birdhouse front. Align paper edge with bottom edge of house. Draw the shape on paper. Draw circles to match doors and place a large dot for perch. Proceed with this method for all four sides. Occasionally wooden products have slight measurement differences from side to side. Cutting a pattern for each side assures a perfect fit.

STEP 3

Cut out pattern shapes and pin to fabric. Be sure print direction matches. Cut out fabric. Cut out door holes. Make a dot for perch placement.

STEP 4

Working in a well-ventilated area, place one fabric piece, facedown, on newspaper. Coat fabric with spray adhesive. Immediately place fabric on birdhouse side and smooth into place. Repeat process for each fabric piece, using a new sheet of newspaper for each.

STEP 5

With hot glue, secure sphagnum moss thickly to roof. Secure sea lavender to front of birdhouse interspersed with lavender spikes. Attach remaining botanicals to the back of birdhouse. With hot glue, attach rosebuds randomly to front.

STEP 6

Use scissors to poke holes in fabric for perches. Press perches into place.

And when thou art weary, I'll find thee a bed of mosses and flowers to pillow thy head...

—JOHN KEATS 1795–1821

NIGELLA HEART WREATH

MATERIALS:

20-26 silica-dried blue nigella

8-10 silica-dried white nigella

3 dried miniature white roses

10-12 spikes dried lavender

Sphagnum moss

1 ¼ yards of ⅝-inch-wide white-with-blue-edging French wired ribbon

1 yard florist's wire

One 3-inch piece florist's wire

Glue gun/glue sticks

STEP 1

With the 34-inch piece of wire, glue gun, and moss, make a moss-covered heart-shaped wreath base approximately 8 inches tall and 9 inches wide (see page 38).

STEP 2

With hot glue, attach nigella, roses, and lavender to front of wreath, distributing materials evenly.

STEP 3

Cut a 6-inch piece of ribbon and set aside. Use remaining ribbon to form a six-loop bow, 4 inches wide overall, with 9-inch streamers (see page 34). Using 3-inch piece of wire, secure bow center. Use remaining 6-inch piece of ribbon to make a 3-inch double-gathered piece. Fold and secure both ends with hot glue (see page 34). Place gathered ribbon section around bow center and secure ends to back of bow with hot glue.

STEP 4

With hot glue, secure bow to upper-left-hand side of wreath.

COUNTRY BASKET

Decorate baskets with printed fabric. The print used in this basket is a French border fabric, narrow strips of prints used to hem tablecloths and skirts. Fabrics printed with floral strips work equally well. Baskets of any size can be used for this project. Measure around your basket to determine fabric length. Add 1 inch for fabric overlap. Measure basket from rim to base, adding ¼ inch to accommodate batting. This will determine the width of the fabric strip.

MATERIALS:

One 12x8x4-inch basket with handle

1 yard 3-inch-wide floral-print fabric

Forest-green acrylic paint

Round brush

Cotton batting

Glue gun/glue sticks

STEP 1

Using round brush, paint entire basket green. Allow paint to dry completely before proceeding.

STEP 2

Wrap fabric strip around basket. Use hot glue to attach bottom edge of fabric to basket just above basket base. Be sure to cover entire edge with glue, smoothing as you glue and leaving no section unglued. Where fabric ends meet, secure together with hot glue to create a seam. Allow glue to set before proceeding.

STEP 3

Gently pack batting evenly into pocket between fabric and basket. With hot glue, secure top edge of fabric to basket.

LITTLE BIRD TOPIARY

MATERIALS:

2 cups miniature red rosebuds

30 sprigs fresh or dried maidenhair fern

1 sturdy 14-inch branch

Sphagnum moss

19 inches aluminum bonsai wire

22 inches aluminum bonsai wire

8 inches aluminum bonsai wire

½ of 9-inch-diameter plastic foam ball

1 square plastic foam cut to fit pot

5x5-inch terra-cotta pot

Glue gun/glue sticks

STEP 1

With hot glue, secure plastic foam in pot. Cover top of foam with moss. Secure in place with hot glue.

STEP 2

To create topiary tree, push one end of branch into flat side of foam-ball half. Push the other end into center of foam in pot.

STEP 3

With hot glue, secure moss to topiary treetop.

STEP 4

Bend the 22-inch piece of wire into the shape of a bird, following pattern. Place wire on pattern and bend to match shape. Twist ends together to secure wire in place. Use 22-inch piece of wire to make wing shapes.

STEP 5

Use 8-inch piece of wire to attach wings to body by twisting it around both pieces to secure. Twist wire ends together and push into top, center point of topiary. With hot glue, secure moss around wires to cover.

STEP 6

Use hot glue to add rosebuds and fern sprigs to topiary and bird. Distribute materials evenly. If fresh ferns are used, they will dry in place.

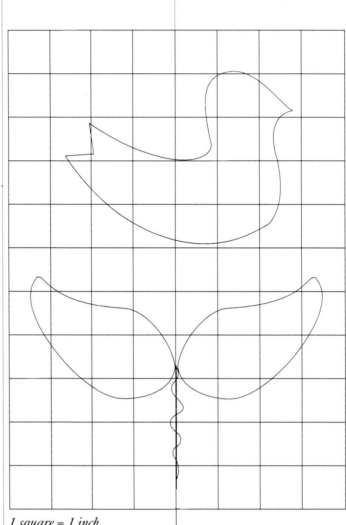

1 square = 1 inch

Planting seeds is like planting magic. No matter how well the spot is marked, there is a shred of doubt as to exactly where the plants will be. The water is added, and we go about our lives. When we remember to go back, there it is— the surprise! Hints of green that will one day become a bouquet.

TEACUP GARDENS

MATERIALS FOR FRESH-FLOWER TEACUP GARDEN:

1 patterned teacup

A selection of small flowers

Sprigs of herbs

Florist's foam cut to fit teacup

Liquid or powdered plant food for cut flowers

STEP 1

Fill a bowl or sink with cool water and add appropriate amount of plant food following manufacturer's directions. Soak florist's foam until liquid has been completely absorbed, usually about 20 minutes.

STEP 2

Place florist's foam in teacup. Arrange sprigs of herbs and flowers in foam. To preserve freshness for a longer period of time, store in the refrigerator overnight.

HERBS AND FLOWERS FOR FRESH TEACUP GARDENS

Baby's breath, Bachelor's button, Columbine, Daisy, Feverfew, Forget-me-not, Lavender, Lily of the valley, Marigold, Miniature daffodil, Miniature rose, Nigella, Pansy, Pink, Primrose, Sweet pea, Sweet william, Verbena

MATERIALS FOR DRIED-FLOWER TEACUP GARDEN:

1 patterned teacup

A selection of small dried botanicals

Florist's dry foam cut to fit teacup

Sphagnum moss

Glue gun/glue sticks

STEP 1

With hot glue, attach foam inside teacup.

STEP 2

Place a small amount of moss on foam to cover. Secure in place with dots of hot glue.

STEP 3

Arrange dried material in teacup. Choose a color theme to complement teacup.

BOTANICALS FOR DRIED-FLOWER TEACUP GARDENS

Baby's breath, Bachelor's button, Bittersweet, Dried herbs, Feverfew, Lavender, Larkspur, Lemon balm, Miniature rose, Parsley, Pepperberries, Poppy pods, Small twigs, Statice, Sweet annie, Tansy, Yarrow

TEABAG LAVENDER SACHET

MATERIALS:

7 inches of 4-inch-wide iridescent teal organdy ribbon

2 tablespoons dried lavender

6 inches white garden string

1 ½ inches of 3-inch-wide provincial-print border fabric

Acrylic matte medium

Round brush

Needle

Iron

Pencil

Tracing paper

Stapler (optional)

STEP 1

Fold organdy ribbon in half lengthwise. Stitch up the side to create a seam.

STEP 2

Turn ribbon right side out. Move seam to the center and press flat. Fold in half again with seam facing upward. Press well.

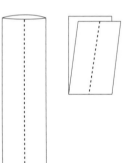

STEP 3

Fold both sides downward ¼ inch from halfway fold. Press folds in place.

STEP 4

Place 1 tablespoon lavender into each side. Fold and press opening. Thread needle with string knotted at one end. Push needle through sachet and allow string to hang freely. Continue folding top of sachet and stitch or staple closed.

STEP 5

To make tag, brush back of fabric with matte medium. Allow to dry. The fabric will become stiff. Trace tea-tag pattern.

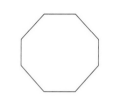

When fabric has dried, cut out two pattern pieces. Glue together with string in between.

POTPOURRI RECIPES

These recipes will yield enough potpourri for 12 teabags with enough left over to display in a small bowl or a basket. For information on how to mix these potpourris, see page 44.

Peppermint Potpourri

1 cup broken peppermint or spearmint leaves

1 cup lavender

½ cup apple-mint leaves

1 tablespoon orrisroot

3 drops peppermint oil

1 drop lavender oil

Spicy Spring Potpourri

2 cups dried, broken lemon verbena leaves

1 cup lavender

½ cup whole cloves

2 tablespoons orrisroot

2 drops lemon oil

2 drops cinnamon oil

2 drops bergamot oil

Rose Lavender Potpourri

2 cups dried lavender

1 cup dried miniature red rose petals

2 tablespoons orrisroot

6 drops lavender oil

3 drops damask rose oil

*Buds open, the garden is filled with youth and hope.
Roses reach full bloom and we are reminded of the cycles of
the year, the cycles of life.*

Gardens grand and gardens small are all made of single flowers tended, watered, and warmed by the sun. Whether we nurture a single miniature rose blooming in an old clay pot on the windowsill or grow beds of amber chrysanthemums, we engage in a partnership with nature.

HONEY ROSE WREATH

MATERIALS:

One 10-inch-diameter wreath of preserved miniature baby's breath

15 freeze-dried Candia roses

8 freeze-dried deep red roses

15-20 dried blue delphinium flowers

4 silica-dried blue asters

10 small bunches dried yarrow

6 dried coreopsis

6 dried blue nigella

15-20 sprigs ornamental oregano

6 small bunches pink yarrow

8 inches florist's wire

Glue gun/glue sticks

STEP 1

With hot glue, secure Candia roses to wreath in groups of two or three. Add deep red roses and other flowers, distributing evenly.

STEP 2

To create a hanger, push wire through back center point of wreath and twist ends together to form a loop.

LITTLE POTPOURRI PACKAGES

MATERIALS:

Three 2 ¾x2x2-inch blocks florist's oasis or plastic foam

1 cup dried, crushed rose petals

1 cup dried sunflower petals

1 cup dried lavender

Three 26-inch pieces natural raffia

Rose, sandalwood, and lavender essential oils

Craft brush

White craft glue

STEP 1

Using brush and working in sections, cover one block with craft glue. Press on rose petals. Continue until all sides have been covered. Allow glue to set before proceeding. Following this procedure, cover another block with sunflower petals and the third block with lavender.

STEP 2

Wrap each block with raffia and tie a single bow (see page 33). Apply a few drops of the appropriate essential oil to each block.

PRESSED-FLOWER CANDLE

MATERIALS:

*One 5 ½x2 ½x2 ½-inch white
pillar candle
Assorted pressed flowers
and leaves
1 white votive candle
Craft brush
Small double boiler and water*

Melt votive candle in top of
double boiler. Working
quickly, use brush to apply
melted wax to back of a
pressed botanical and place
immediately on candle.
Continue in this manner
until candle has been
decorated. A thin coat of
wax may then be painted
over botanical
for protection.

BEE SKEP

MATERIALS:

*One 6x5-inch-diameter bee
skep with artificial bees
1 bamboo plate holder
Sphagnum moss
5 small bunches dried yarrow
3 small bunches dried acacia
4 silica-dried
miniature daisies
2 silica-dried violas
1 silica-dried white rose*

*17 dried larkspur flowers
One 6-inch stem blue
delphinium
4-5 sprigs preserved
miniature baby's breath
1 stem white yarrow
12 stems dried acacia leaves
1 stem dried Paprika yarrow
1 coreopsis
3 wispy twigs
Glue gun/glue sticks*

STEP 1

Turn bamboo plate holder
upside down. With hot
glue, cover thickly with
moss to create a base.
With hot glue, secure bee
skep to left-hand side of
base. Secure moss around
base of skep.

STEP 2

With hot glue, attach white
yarrow stem behind the
left-hand side of skep.
Attach delphinium stem in
front of the white yarrow.
Secure remaining flowers
and leaves around skep to
create a garden effect.

*The Pedigree of Honey Does not concern the Bee—
A Clover, any time, to him, Is Aristocracy.*

EMILY DICKENSON
1830–1886

A garden path, slightly overgrown with heather and lamb's ear winds past honeysuckle and angelica to a bench of worn green paint. This gardening season, create a quiet hideaway for reading and writing to friends.

PINK STRAW-FLOWER WREATH

MATERIALS:

One 12-inch straw wreath

20-24 dried pink strawflowers

15-20 dried white strawflowers

100 small dried red rosebuds

Dried melaleuca or bay leaves

2 yards of 1 ½-inch-wide dusty rose with celery-green striped French wired ribbon

12 inches florist's wire

Glue gun/glue sticks

STEP 1

With hot glue, secure leaves around outer edges of wreath base. Leaves should point outward from wreath base.

STEP 2

With hot glue, attach white and pink strawflowers to center of wreath, distributing evenly and alternating colors and sizes. With hot glue, secure rosebuds among flowers.

STEP 3

Cut ribbon into two 36-inch pieces. Pull the wire along one edge of one ribbon piece to ruffle (see page 33). Using this ribbon, make a double bow (see page 34). The first bow should be 6 inches wide overall, the second, 5 ½ inches wide overall. Use remaining ribbon to form two streamers. Trim streamers in an inverted V shape. Shape bow with fingers and attach to the lower-right-hand side of wreath. Streamers may be glued into place.

STEP 4

Form a hanger by threading florist's wire through top center point on back of wreath and twisting ends together to form a loop.

HEATHER BASKET

MATERIALS:

One 4x6-inch bark basket with handle

1 bunch silver artemisia

1 bunch deep pink heather

Sphagnum moss

Green acrylic paint

Round brush

Glue gun/glue sticks

STEP 1

With brush and green paint, paint basket rim and base. Allow paint to dry completely before proceeding.

STEP 2

With hot glue, attach alternating stems of artemisia and heather to sides of basket. Place plant material on a diagonal until basket is covered in pink and silver stripes. With hot glue, attach moss to top rim and basket base to cover stems.

"As is the garden such is the gardener. A man's nature runs either to herbs or weeds."

—FRANCIS BACON,
1561–1626

PRESSED-FLOWER PLATE

Pressed flowers have many applications. Creating plates to display on the wall or tabletops is both easy to do and satisfying. Make several plates in colors that have been coordinated with your decor and hang them as a grouping. These plates are for display only, however they can be cleaned by wiping with a damp cloth.

MATERIALS:

One 8-inch-diameter clear-glass plate

Selection of small pressed flowers and leaves

Acrylic gloss medium

Light and dark blue acrylic paint (or colors of choice)

Round brush

Sheet of white paper

STEP 1

Place sheet of white paper on flat work surface. Turn plate upside down on center of paper. Place pressed flowers on white paper or near at hand. Working with one flower or leaf at a time, apply an even coat of gloss medium to front of flower or leaf. Place immediately on plate. Continue with gloss medium and individual botanicals until a pleasing design has been achieved. Allow approximately 20 minutes for gloss medium to dry.

STEP 2

With round brush, apply an even coat of gloss medium to entire back of plate, covering wrong side of flowers and leaves. Allow gloss medium to dry completely. Apply an even, second coat of the gloss medium. Allow gloss medium to dry for approximately 20 minutes before proceeding.

STEP 3

With round brush, apply an even coat of dark blue paint to center area of plate. Apply an even coat of light blue paint to outer band of plate. Allow paint to dry completely before proceeding. Apply a second coat of the same color to each area.

STEP 4

Apply a final coat of gloss medium to entire back of plate. Cover all painted areas. Allow gloss medium to dry for approximately 20 minutes.

BOTANICALS TO PRESS FOR PLATES

Baby's breath, Calendula petals, Forget-me-not, Individual stock flowers, Ivy leaves, Maidenhair fern, Miniature rose petals, Mint leaves, Nasturtium, Nigella, Pansy, Primrose, Small daisy, Small narcissus, Small rose leaves, Sunflower petals, Viola, Violet

ROSEBUD AND RIBBON LAMPSHADE

MATERIALS:

One 4x4-inch-diameter lampshade

26 inches of 4-inch-wide deep purple French wired ribbon

Glue gun/glue sticks

STEP 1

Gather wired ribbon at top and bottom edges until length will cover lampshade completely with a ½-inch overlap (see page 34).

STEP 2

With hot glue, secure ribbon to lampshade at top and bottom edges. Overlap ends by ¼ inch, securing with hot glue.

STEP 3

Make a beaded garland for shade using the following instructions. Glue garland on a diagonal on front of shade.

WOODEN BEAD MINI GARLAND

MATERIALS:

1 ½ yards of 1-inch-wide deep purple French wired ribbon

Eight ½-inch-diameter wooden beads

20-26 miniature red or pink rosebuds

7 sprigs baby's breath

Toothpicks

STEP 1

Push ribbon through one bead to within 1 inch of ribbon end.

Bring long ribbon end down over and back up through bead.

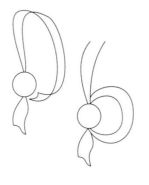

Spread ribbon over bead and pull end through. Repeat, threading long ribbon section through bead until entire bead surface has been covered. Three wraps will usually cover a bead. Use toothpick to push ribbon end through bead on the third wrap, as bead hole will become narrow.

STEP 2

Add next bead to ribbon and repeat Step 1. Continue until all eight beads have been covered and strung.

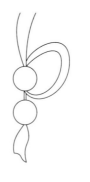

STEP 3

With hot glue, secure rosebuds between beads. Attach baby's breath in between the roses to finish garland.

RUFFLED NOSEGAY

MATERIALS:

3 small preserved pink roses

9 dried rose leaves

4 dried larkspur flowers

4 small sprigs silica-dried forget-me-nots

1 yard of 1 ½-inch-wide blue ombre wired ribbon

¾ yard of ⅝-inch-wide black-edged, deep purple wired ribbon

Small amount sphagnum moss

Pinking or scalloping shears

4 inches florist's wire

Glue gun/glue sticks

STEP 1

Using deep purple ribbon, make a six-loop bow (see page 34) with two 2-inch streamers. Finish streamers by cutting at an angle with pinking or scalloping shears. Set bow aside.

STEP 2

Gather one edge of blue ombre ribbon to form a ruffle (see page 33). Fold extended wire end of gathered ribbon over on itself. Press gently to secure wire. With hot glue, secure fold in place. Trim excess wire.

STEP 3

Hold one end of ribbon. Form a 4-inch-diameter circle (center hole will be approximately 2 inches in diameter). Continue placing ruffled ribbon length around circle, matching hole size, until a second ruffled layer is achieved. With hot glue, secure inner edges together around center hole.

STEP 4

With hot glue, attach moss to center of ribbon circle. Attach rose leaf stems to moss, allowing leaves to stand upright around mossed center. Into leaf cup attach roses, larkspur, and forget-me-nots.

STEP 5

To finish, secure bow to bottom of nosegay ruffle with hot glue. Edges of bow should just peek out.

MOSSY ROSE NOSEGAY

MATERIALS:

1 dried or freeze-dried white rose

30 miniature dried red rosebuds

8 small dried pink rosebuds

4 dried globe amaranth

1 stalk silica-dried blue delphiniums

4 dried small daisies

1 stalk purple larkspur

6 sprigs pink heather

Small handful dried sea lavender

1-2 sprigs dried white baby's breath

7-8 dried rose leaves

One handful sphagnum moss

Small amount oakmoss

Damask rose oil (optional)

One 5-inch-diameter piece cardboard, 1-inch center circle cut out

Glue gun/glue sticks

STEP 1

With hot glue, secure sphagnum moss thickly to both sides of cardboard. Glue white rose to center of moss on top side. Surround white rose with small dried pink rosebuds and secure in place with hot glue.

STEP 2

With hot glue, add the remaining greenery, ferns, and flowers to the nosegay, distributing evenly.

FLORAL JEWELRY

Each season presents us with precious jewels from the garden. Sapphire hyacinths, amber-centered daisies, emerald leaves of ivy, all blooming in their season, can be gathered and fashioned into pins and necklaces. Wear ruby rosebuds for all romantic occasions.

FAN PIN

MATERIALS:

1 brass fan charm

3 dried red or pink miniature rosebuds

3 dried boxwood leaves

12 inches of 1/16-inch-wide antique burgundy silk ribbon

Several sprigs fir

1 pin back

Glue gun/glue sticks

STEP 1

With hot glue, secure boxwood leaves to center point of fan charm. Attach rosebuds to leaves.

STEP 2

With red ribbon, make a small single bow with long streamers. Secure to fan charm just below rosebuds. Add fir sprigs.

STEP 3

With hot glue, attach pin back to back of charm.

OVAL PIN

Foam-covered shapes with adhesive backings are perfect for jewelry making. Shapes are available in ovals and hearts. The supplier for these forms can be found in the Resource Guide on page 162.

MATERIALS:

One 2 1/2x1 7/8-inch foam-covered oval with adhesive back

4x3-inch oval scrap of provincial-print trim fabric

8 inches of 1/4-inch-wide gold braid

8 dried miniature red or pink rosebuds

8 dried boxwood leaves

6 dried feverfew flowers

Piece of felt cut to fit oval (color of choice)

1 pin back

Scissors

Glue gun/glue sticks

STEP 1

Cut fabric scrap according to pattern supplied by the manufacturer of oval foam shape. Position fabric piece on oval and press edges around to backing. Adhesive on back of oval shape will hold fabric in place. With hot glue, secure gold braid around the edge of oval.

STEP 2

With hot glue, secure boxwood leaves to center of oval in a sunburst pattern. Attach rosebuds to leaves, forming a small bouquet. Fill gaps with feverfew.

STEP 3

Secure felt oval to back of decorated oval, covering fabric edges. Secure pin back to back of oval with hot glue.

GOLDEN BOUQUET PIN

MATERIALS:

One 4-inch-square brass wire mesh

12 inches of 1/16-inch-wide antique lilac silk ribbon

1 stem dried purple larkspur

1 pin back

Glue gun/glue sticks

STEP 1

Fold over 1/4-inch edges of mesh square.

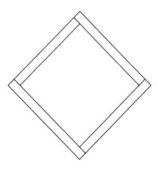

Fold into a cone shape. Pull back the two inside corners.

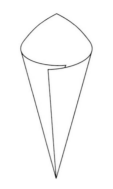

STEP 2

With hot glue, secure the midpoint of ribbon to the center back of cone. Criss-cross ribbon around the cone until the bottom point is reached. Secure ribbon with dots of hot glue. Finish with a small single bow.

STEP 3

With hot glue, attach pin back to back of cone. Fill cone with dried flowers, secured in place with hot glue.

ROMANTIC ROSE PIN

MATERIALS:

12 inches 1 1/2-inch purple French wired satin ribbon

3 dried red rosebuds

6 dried miniature red rosebuds

Several small sprigs baby's breath

Several small sprigs fir

1 pin back

Scissors

Glue gun/glue sticks

STEP 1

Tie a loose double knot in the middle of ribbon. Secure the large rosebuds to center of knot. With hot glue, attach two of the miniature rosebuds above the larger roses. Attach remaining miniature rosebuds below the larger roses.

STEP 2

With hot glue, secure few sprigs of baby's breath and fir around roses. Trim ribbon streamers to desired length. Secure pin back to ribbon back with hot glue.

FRENCH COUNTRY BUTTON COVER

MATERIALS:

1 1/2-inch metal button cover

6 inches deep green pleated French wired ribbon

Scrap of provincial-print border fabric

13 dried pink or red miniature rosebuds

Needle and coordinating thread

Wire cutter

Glue gun/glue sticks

STEP 1

Gather one edge of pleated ribbon and pull tightly (see page 33). Trim wire and stitch raw edges together. Fan gathered ribbon out to form a circle. With hot glue, attach ribbon circle to button cover.

STEP 2

Cover button blank with fabric according to manufacturer's instructions. Secure covered button to center of gathered ribbon circle with hot glue.

STEP 3

With hot glue, attach rosebuds around button.

RIBBON AND ROSES BARRETTE

MATERIALS:

14 inches of 1 ½-inch-wide purple French wired ribbon

14 inches of ½-inch-wide gold-edged lilac organza ribbon

1 metal hair clip

4 dried miniature red or pink rosebuds

4 dried boxwood leaves

Several small sprigs baby's breath

STEP 1

Align edges of both pieces of ribbon. Tie five loose knots along the length of purple ribbon, spacing knots close together. Fold ribbon ends under and secure in place with hot glue.

STEP 2

With hot glue, secure knotted ribbons to hair clip. Gather as needed to fit on clip. Attach rosebuds to ribbon knots with hot glue. Secure boxwood leaves just below rosebuds.

ROSE BEAD NECKLACE

MATERIALS:

Heavy white thread

Embroidery needle

Generous handful dried rose petals

61 small gold beads

83 miniature red rosebuds

White craft glue

Small bowl

Sheet waxed paper

Water with a few drops of rose oil to moisten hands

Materials listed make a strand approximately 34 inches long.

STEP 1

Place rose petals in bowl. Add small amount of glue. Moisten hands in water and mascerate glue and rose petals until petals and glue are well blended. Add glue to petals as necessary. Roll approximately one teaspoon of mixture between palms forming small beads. Place beads on waxed paper to dry. Allow glue to set two hours.

STEP 2

Thread needle. Begin stringing rose beads, rosebuds and gold beads, alternating to create a pleasing pattern. Tie thread ends together in a double knot when necklace reaches desired length.

SUMMER GARDEN PROJECTS

Each garden seems to have a spirit of its own, imparted in part by its caretaker. Plants grow, flourish, and bloom, adding a life of their own. Visiting bees and butterflies, ladybirds and toads help pollinate and tend. And then there are the fairies... In Ireland, the delicate little bells of lily of the valley have been thought of as fairy ladders for the "little people" to climb.

—FOLKLORE

OVAL WREATH OF SUMMER FLOWERS

MATERIALS:

1 yard aluminum bonsai wire

7-10 small dried pink and cream roses

7-10 dried blue delphiniums

7-10 dried pink globe amaranth

10-12 pink and white strawflowers

7-10 dried pinks

Selection of small filler flowers

Sphagnum moss

Glue gun/glue sticks

Bend wire into a circle. To secure, twist 2 inches of ends together. Bend circle into an oval shape. With glue gun, work in sections and cover entire wire with moss. Attach flowers to wreath, mixing colors and varieties. Wreath may be scented by adding a few drops of essential oil to moss.

So often flower arrangements, like gardens, are planned for blended color transitions: pink near mauve, with accents of rose and violet.

The colors melt into one another in harmony and the eye is pleased.

But the boldness of orange next to purple, reds placed beside magenta, is somehow more exciting, like paintings of pure pigment, freely applied, and we are left breathless.

ROSEBUD POMANDERS

MATERIALS FOR ONE POMANDER:

One 3-inch-diameter plastic foam ball

2 cups potpourri (recipe of choice)

14 inches aluminum bonsai wire

2 cups red, pink, or variegated miniature rosebuds

Selection of lichen, oakmoss, Spanish moss, sphagnum moss

6-8 small pieces of cinnamon sticks

Waxed paper

Blender

White craft glue

Bowl

Glue gun/glue sticks

STEP 1

Remove hard materials such as cinnamon sticks, whole allspice, whole cloves, and nutmegs from potpourri. Place remaining potpourri in blender and grind until pieces are small. Place potpourri in bowl. Cover entire ball with white craft glue. Roll ball in ground potpourri until completely covered.
Set ball on waxed paper. Allow glue to set before proceeding.

STEP 2

Bend wire into hanger shape. Press wire ends into ball. Secure with a small amount of hot glue around base of wire.

STEP 3

With hot glue, attach mosses, twigs, and rose-buds around wire base to form a crown. With hot glue, secure a band of sphagnum or oakmoss around pomander.
Add rosebuds, twigs, and cinnamon pieces to decorate.

GARDEN TOPIARY

This topiary is arranged with fresh materials and allowed to dry in place.

MATERIALS:

One 5x5 ½-inch-diameter terra-cotta pot

Florist's foam cut to fit pot

16 stems oregano

4 stems sweet marjoram

6 stems thyme

10 sprigs ornamental oregano

3-5 scabious

5-6 globe amaranth

6-7 sage flowers

2-3 monarda blooms

4-5 stems blue salvia

8-10 stems lavender

1 dill flower head

10-12 Cupid's darts

4-6 small bay leaves

Sphagnum moss

Pumpkin powdered-milk paint

Light moss-green acrylic paint

Water

Round brush

2 ½ yards aluminum bonsai wire

Wire cutters

Glue gun/glue sticks

STEP 1

Using round brush and green paint, paint exterior of flowerpot. Allow paint to dry completely before proceeding. Mix powdered-milk paint with water, following manufacturer's instructions. Paint over green paint with milk paint, using free-flowing strokes and allowing small amounts of green paint to show through. The effect will be a chalky, aged look. Allow paint to dry completely before proceeding.

STEP 2

Bend wire length in half. Twist free ends together to create a double wire approximately 1 ¼ yards long. Bend wire to form a figure-eight shape. Top circle should be slightly smaller than bottom circle. Twist ends together to form a straight, 3-inch piece used to anchor topiary in pot. Press anchor piece into foam and secure with hot glue. Cover base with moss and secure in place with hot glue.

STEP 3

Press four oregano stems into foam at base of wire form. Wind oregano around wire. Working with single herb and flower stems, continue weaving herbs and flowers around wire to cover. Begin each stem by tucking it into herb stems already in place. These will stay in place as fresh stems are flexible.

STEP 4

On front of topiary form, at base of topiary and intersection of circles, attach blossoms and flowers in a random, pleasing pattern. Use hot glue to secure in place if necessary. Push several flower stems into the moss in front of topiary and secure with hot glue. Attach bay leaves where desired to add height and fill in gaps.

FLOWER FAIRY

MATERIALS:

Air-dry white craft modeling clay

10 inches 3-inch-wide yellow organdy ribbon

Two 2-inch-wide pieces lavender organdy ribbon

Handful potpourri or lavender

¼ yard 3-inch-wide scalloped organdy ribbon petals, gathered

Small amount Spanish moss

2 silica-dried white tulip petals

1 silica-dried peach rose, fully opened

2 sprigs small artificial silk lilacs

1 tablespoon dried calendula petals

12 inches heavy-gauge florist's wire

Black, white, blue, raspberry, and unbleached titanium acrylic paint

Round brush

Fine-line brush

Toothpick

Lavender and yellow thread and needle

Wire cutter

Needle nose pliers

Glue gun/glue sticks

STEP 1

To form head, roll clay into a 2-inch-diameter ball. Pinch into shape, leaving an extra-long portion at bottom for neck. Form eye indentations by pressing forefingers into face. Set aside to dry.

STEP 2

To form arms, roll clay into two 2 ½-inch-long coils, ¼ inch in diameter. Pinch into shape at shoulder and hands. Bend at elbows. Use a toothpick to delineate thumbs and fingers. Set aside to dry.

STEP 3

To form legs, roll clay into two 3 ½-inch coils slightly thicker than arm pieces. Pinch into shape at top and foot. Bend knee on one leg. Set aside to dry.

I know a little garden close, Set thickly with lily and red rose. Where I would wander if I might From dewy morn to dewy night.

WILLIAM MORRIS
1834–1896

STEP 4

When clay pieces have dried, they can be painted. With fine-line brush and acrylic paints, paint eye ovals white. Paint irises blue with a pin dot of black paint. A tiny white highlight may be added to black pupil. Use black for lining eyes and delineating lashes. Overlap the very top of the blue irises with black liner. Paint three small dots of raspberry for lips. Line and fill in dots. Add a white highlight to the lower lip.

Blend raspberry and unbleached titanium until the desired cheek color is achieved. Paint on cheek area. Dot a tiny amount on tip of nose and chin. Set pieces aside.

STEP 5

To form the body, fold the 10-inch piece of ribbon in half lengthwise. Sew length and one end close to ribbon edge to create a pouch, leaving top open. Turn right side out. Fold 1 inch of ribbon down from top. Sew a running stitch all the way around and do not tie off. Fill ribbon bag with potpourri or lavender. Place fairy's neck inside opening and gather fabric tightly, using needle and thread still in place to create a ruff. Secure ruff to neck with dots of hot glue.

STEP 6

Use wire cutter to cut wire piece in half. One piece will be used to join fairy's arms to body; the other piece will join her legs to her body. Push one wire through one arm and into the body, passing through the lower neck, out of the body, and into the other arm. Push arms close to body and cut wire ends to extend ½ inch beyond arms. Use needle nose pliers to twist each wire end to form a small loop. These loops will secure arms in place .

STEP 7

Repeat the process of Step 6 to attach fairy's legs to her body. Pass wire through top of one leg, sachet body, and remaining leg. Trim and twist wires to secure legs in place.

STEP 8

Fold a 2-inch piece of lavender ribbon in half. With needle and lavender thread, gather raw ends together and knot off. Sew tuft just under neck ruff at shoulder. Repeat for other side.

STEP 9

To form the skirt, glue the scalloped organdy ribbon around the waist. Gently remove petals from peach rose. With hot glue, attach petals one by one to body just above organdy skirt ribbon. Use hot glue to attach calendula petals around waistline at point where rose petals are glued.

STEP 10

With hot glue, attach artificial flowers to fairy's head to frame her face. Glue wisps of moss to head for hair. To form wings, use hot glue to attach tulip petals to fairy's back.

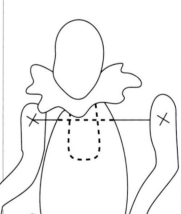

SUNFLOWER TABLE

MATERIALS:

One 3 ½-inch-diameter air-dried sunflower

Three 2 ½-inch twigs for legs

One 1 ½-inch Y-shaped twig for leg brace

Glue gun/glue sticks

STEP 1

Make tableleg assembly by attaching Y-shaped twig to midway point of the three 2½-inch twigs with dots of hot glue. This will create a brace between three legs.

STEP 2

Use hot glue to attach leg assembly to underside of sunflower.

DAFFODIL LAMP

MATERIALS:

One AA battery holder with battery

1 dried poppy pod for lamp base

1 silica-dried daffodil

1 dollhouse light-bulb assembly

Darning needle

Glue gun/glue sticks

STEP 1

Use darning needle and gently make a hole in poppy pod large enough to accommodate dollhouse light bulb. Thread light bulb and wire through hole and fasten bulb in an upright position above pod to create a lamp.

STEP 2

With hot glue, attach daffodil upside down over bulb. Secure lamp to tabletop and attach wires to battery holder.

TWIG FURNITURE

The twigs used for this project are from a ficus tree. Choose twigs that have many small offshoots and tendrils. The twigs of a ficus are also naturally pliable.

MATERIALS:

One 2 1/2-inch-long twig for front leg

One 11-12-inch-long U-shaped twig for chair back and legs

One 10-inch-long twig for seat

Three 2-inch-long thin twigs for leg braces

Assorted small twigs

Spool of florist's wire

Spanish moss

Garden clippers

Hot water

Large bowl

Wire cutter

STEP 1

Fill bowl with hot water and soak twigs for 20 to 30 minutes. Soaking will render twigs more pliable for bending. Leave any thin tendrils on twigs, as these will be useful for weaving in chair seat and chair back.

STEP 2

Remove 10-inch twig from water and bend into a rough oval shape. Secure twig ends together with a twist of wire. Wire will be covered with moss after twigs dry. Weave small tendrils from twig in and out through the center of oval shape to create a chair seat.

STEP 3

Remove U-shaped twig and leg piece from water and allow to dry for fifteen minutes. With hot glue, attach small twig to oval using hot glue. With hot glue, attach U-shaped twig to opposite side of oval to form back of chair and two back legs. Glue three thin twigs midway between seat and leg bottoms as braces.

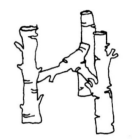

STEP 4

With hot glue, attach small twigs across center of seat oval and center of back. Use bits of moss to cover hot glue joints.

*A thing of beauty
is a joy for ever:
Its loveliness
increases:
it will never
Pass into
nothingness;
but still will keep
A bower quiet
for us,...*
JOHN KEATS,
1795–1821

ELEGANT ROSE TOPIARY

MATERIALS:

One 10x6x6 embossed white porcelain container with handles

Plastic foam cut to fit in pot

One 12-inch sturdy tree branch

One-half 12-inch-diameter plastic foam ball

Large amount sphagnum moss

8 dried or freeze-dried white roses

12 freeze-dried Candia roses

10 silica-dried purple fuchsia

10 silica-dried miniature pink and purple fuchsias

2 ½ yards of 1-inch-wide green-and-fuchsia-striped French wired ribbon

1 yard of 1-inch-wide fuchsia with green-striped French wired ribbon

Glue gun/glue sticks

STEP 1

With hot glue, secure foam cut to fit container inside pot. Insert one end of branch into flat side of plastic foam ball. Secure with hot glue. Insert opposite end of branch into foam in container. Secure with hot glue. Cover with moss and secure with hot glue. Cover plastic foam ball with moss and secure with hot glue.

STEP 2

Cut the fuchsia ribbon with green stripe into 6-inch pieces. Tie a single knot in the center of each piece. Finish ends in an inverted V shape. Cut the green-and-fuchsia-striped ribbon into one 22-inch piece and the rest into 4-inch pieces. Tie a single knot in the center of the 4-inch pieces. Finish ends in an inverted V shape. Set ribbons aside.

STEP 3

With hot glue, secure roses and fuchsias to mossed topiary, distributing evenly. Fill in gaps with knotted ribbons, scrunching some ribbon ends to vary the pattern. Tie the 22-inch piece of ribbon around the topiary stem and make a single bow, 4 inches wide overall with 6-inch streamers. Finish streamers in an inverted V shape.

ROSEBUD WREATHS

MATERIALS FOR ONE WREATH:

One 3-inch willow wreath base

1 ½ cups miniature rosebuds

One 3-inch piece florist's wire

Glue gun/glue sticks

Use glue gun to attach rosebuds to front and sides of wreath base, leaving no gaps. To form hanger, thread wire through willow on wreath back and twist ends together.

HERB-ROSEBUD SACHET

MATERIALS:

16 inches of 4 1/2-inch-wide moss-green French wired ribbon

2 yards of 1/8-inch-wide pink antique silk ribbon

1 yard of 1/8-inch-wide rose antique silk ribbon

2 yards of 1/8-inch-wide celery-green antique silk ribbon

16 inches of 5/8-inch-wide pink-and-green-striped French wired ribbon

2 straight pins

Handful potpourri

Embroidery needle

Glue gun/glue sticks

STEP 1

Fold ribbon to determine center point. Mark with a straight pin. Measure 4 inches from pin in one direction and mark point with another pin. Thread needle with antique pink ribbon. Make 10 or 11 randomly spaced French knots in the area between the pins.

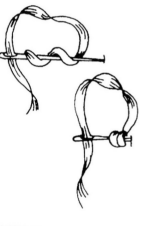

STEP 2

Thread needle with antique rose ribbon. Fill in the spaces between pink French knots with rose French knots. Thread needle with antique green ribbon. Make two loose, straight stitches approximately 1/4 inch in length next to each French knot. Remove straight pins from ribbon.

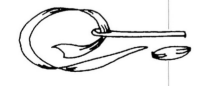

STEP 3

Place ribbon piece on flat surface, wrong side up. Fold 1 inch of each end back over itself onto to wrong side and secure with hot glue. With rosebuds facing outward, match top edges of ribbon and fold in half. Use a thin line of hot glue to secure sides together. This will create a pouch.

STEP 4

Fill pouch with potpourri. Tie closed with the pink-and-green-striped ribbon. Make a single bow and finish streamers in an inverted V shape.

PINK FLORAL SACHET

French border fabric is available in myriad provincial floral prints and colors. When purchasing, be sure to choose a length that allows for print placement on the finished product. A source for these French border prints is listed in the Resource Guide on page 162.

MATERIALS:

16 inches of 4-inch-wide pink-and-white floral print French border fabric

One 8x7-inch piece white or pink fabric

Handful potpourri

1 ⅛ yards of ⅝-inch-wide pink ombre French wired ribbon

One 3-inch piece florist's wire

Coordinating thread and needle

Iron

Scissors

Wire cutter

Glue gun/glue sticks

STEP 1

Cut a 16-inch piece of ribbon. Gather both sides along wires (see page 34). Secure ends with hot glue and trim excess wire. Cut a 20-inch piece of ribbon and form a single bow of gathered ribbon (see page 34). Secure bow center with a twist of craft wire. Use remaining ribbon to gather and glue around bow center. With hot glue, secure bow to center point of gathered ribbon strip. Set aside.

STEP 2

Cut border fabric in half to create two 8-inch pieces. The floral motif should be centered on each piece. Sew pieces together on the wrong side, along the 8-inch side. Center bow and glue ribbon strip to right side of fabric.

STEP 3

With right sides of the fabric together, sew three sides of rectangle to create a pouch with a ½-inch seam allowance. Turn pouch right side out and press along sides to smooth seams. Do not iron ribbon areas.

STEP 4

Fill pouch with potpourri. Turn raw edges of open side inward. Press in place and stitch closed.

ROSY PINK POTPOURRI

MATERIALS:

2 cups pink rose petals

1 cup pink carnation petals

2 cups pink larkspur

1 cup miniature pink rose petals

2 tablespoons orrisroot

6 drops jasmine oil

3 drops French lavender oil

To make potpourri, see page 44.

LEMON WREATH

MATERIALS:

One 9-inch heart-shaped wire wreath

1 yard of 1 ½-inch-wide yellow-with-blue-edge French wired ribbon

9 slices dried lemon

Handful dried lemon and orange peel, cut into small pieces

4 silica-dried daisies

11 white globe amaranth

3 yellow-orange strawflowers

3 sprigs flaxseed pods or commercially dyed green pods

Small amount reindeer moss

Small amount lichen

30-35 dried lemon verbena leaves

7 sprigs lemon verbena flowers

2 inches florist's wire

Glue gun/glue sticks

STEP 1

With hot glue, attach moss, lemon verbena leaves, flowers, and several lemon slices to wreath. Layer materials, adding daisies and other flowers last.

STEP 2

Make a triple bow, 3 ½ inches wide overall, with 7-inch streamers (see page 34). Trim streamer ends in an inverted V shape. With hot glue, secure bow to wreath. Twirl streamers and secure to wreath.

LEMON SACHETS

MATERIALS:

16 inches of 4-inch-wide green-shaded-to-yellow ombre French wired ribbon

Crushed, dried lemon verbena

Cotton batting

Coordinating thread and needle

Pencil

Tracing paper

Straight pins

LEMON-BLEND POTPOURRI

2 cups dried lemon verbena leaves

1 cup dried lemon peel

1 cup dried lemon thyme

1 cup lemon-scented geranium leaves

1 ½ tablespoons orrisroot

8 drops lemon oil

To make potpourri, see instructions on page 44.

STEP 1

Trace pattern onto tracing paper. Cut out pattern shape and pin pattern onto ribbon, covering as much yellow as possible. Cut out four pieces.

STEP 2

Match edges of two of cutout pieces, right sides together, green to green, yellow to yellow. Stitch pieces together ⅛ inch from edge, using a ⅛-inch seam allowance. Leave a 2-inch opening on one seam. Turn right side out.

STEP 3

Stuff with batting and lemon verbena. Stitch opening closed. Cut three leaves from leftover ribbon scraps using leaf pattern. With hot glue, secure leaves to one end of sachet. Repeat process with second set of ribbon pieces.

Leave open on ⎯ one side for adding pot-pourri.

*Remember quiet
summer afternoons,
cooling lemonade on
the porch, and
bunches of fresh
flowers in jam jars
on the windowsill?
Plant daisies along
a picket fence for the
most carefree
welcome
of all.*

HERBAL CARDS

reeting cards and gift tags are especially personal when made by hand, with petals and leaves added from the garden. Notepaper of recycled paper, tied in ribbon and scented with rose oil, are thoughtful and environmentally conscious gifts.

Follow the instructions on page 95 for making sheets of paper. It is during the pulling process that card designs are best executed.

A halfway mark can be placed on the top of your deckle frame with enamel or waterproof paint. This will denote where the paper sheet will be folded to make a greeting card. Materials may be pressed into half of the wet sheet to decorate the card front or may be used over the entire card.

MATERIALS TO PRESS INTO WET PAPER SHEETS:

Cutout wrapping paper flowers, Dried miniature rose petals, Glitter, Herb sprigs, Metallic threads, Mosses, Narrow silk ribbon, Organza ribbon, Pieces of colored craft tissue, Pieces of construction paper, Pieces of embroidery floss, Pressed ferns, Pressed flowers, Pressed leaves, Pressed petals, Scraps of Victorian papers, Small paper doilies, Tiny pearl buttons

Envelopes in many sizes and colors are available through stationery and office-supply stores to fit handmade cards.

Cut herbal papers into heart shapes or small squares for gift tags. Use a single-hole punch to place a hole in one corner of the paper. Thread a narrow ribbon through and tie to gift.

Try spattering acrylic paint over the surface of a sheet of paper. Dip the bristles of a stiff paintbrush into paint. Move brush over paper while running the edge of a knife or piece of cardboard over bristles. Or you can fill a plastic spray bottle with a mixture of water and acrylic paint or water-based ink and spray the paper. Try using both techniques with different colors.

Looking through the study window to the courtyard garden, where mounds of lavender are buzzing with bees, sweet scents waft in and we are transported to the sister gardens of England.

PRESSED-FLOWER KEEPSAKE BOX

Small pressed flowers, petals, and leaves can be used on many decorative glass objects. As botanicals and paint are viewed through the clear, glossy surface of glass, they take on an enameled look. Though small flowers are most suitable for this process, larger petals, such as rose, cosmos, and sunflower can be dried separately and used singly or affixed to larger projects in flower shapes. Acrylic mediums can be purchased in art-supply stores and some crafts shops. The supplier of the gloss medium used in these pressed-flower projects is listed in the Resource Guide on page 162. The medium should not come into contact with food products. Containers decorated in this manner should not be filled with liquid, as the medium could soften and the paint might peel away.

MATERIALS FOR ONE BOX:

1 small six-sided glass-and-brass box with lid

Selection of small pressed flowers, petals, and leaves

Blue acrylic paint

Acrylic gloss medium

Round brush

STEP 1

With brush, apply an even coat of gloss medium to interior of one panel of glass. Place dried botanicals, facedown, onto center of panel. Add petals and leaves as desired while medium is wet. Continue in this manner until all panels and box lid have pressed materials into place. Allow medium approximately 20 minutes to dry.

STEP 2

Apply a second coat of medium to all panels. Brush over the back of botanicals. Allow medium approximately 20 minutes to dry.

STEP 3

With brush and paint, paint panel interior surfaces with an even coat of blue paint. Allow paint to dry completely before proceeding. Apply a second coat of paint. When second coat has dried, apply a final coat of gloss medium. Allow to dry completely before handling.

ADDITIONAL GLASS ITEMS FOR PRESSED FLOWER DECOUPAGE

Clear Christmas balls, Dry flower vases, Decorative bottles, Hollow-glass lamp bases, Paperweights, Picture liners, Potpourri bowls, Tabletops, Trays

HERBAL RAFFIA BOW

MATERIALS:

1 package of 2-yard lengths natural raffia

Five 4x3-inch-diameter natural twig baskets with handles

Sphagnum moss

Florist's moist foam cut to fit each basket

Aluminum foil

Large selection of 6-inch fresh herb cuttings

Scissors

STEP 1

Soak all pieces of florist's foam in water for approximately 20 minutes. Line all baskets with aluminum foil. Place wet foam inside baskets.

STEP 2

Place moss on top of foam. Fill each basket with a pretty arrangement of mixed herb cuttings. Push stems well into moist foam. Set aside.

STEP 3

Lay raffia flat. Make a single bow, 10 inches wide overall, with 27-inch streamers.

STEP 4

Tie baskets onto strands of raffia at uneven lengths.

PAPERMAKING

ecycling is a part of everyday life for the gardener; leaves and clippings are composted to create the rich soil for next year's flowers. Crafters, too, recycle materials that are often discarded to create imaginative projects that add beauty to the home. Fabric scraps become treasured heirloom quilts, and bits of ribbon and lace are transformed into keepsake ornaments for the Christmas tree. Paper, too, can easily turn into handmade cards and notepaper, rich in herbal scent and texture.

The experimentation required to create this book yielded many delightful discoveries, but none was more fun than papermaking. In the kitchen, with readily available materials, papers set aside for the recycling bin, including brown-paper grocery bags, were transformed into hand-made papers full of tiny rose petals and herbs, much like those found in art stores and card shops. This is a project that children and teens will also enjoy. In addition, it is a perfect class project to teach recycling as it happens before one's very eyes!

Glossary of Papermaking Terms

Couching The action of transferring a sheet of newly made paper from the mold to a damp felt piece or towel for drying.

Deckle The frame that fits on top of the mold and determines the size of a sheet of paper. Deckle is also used to describe the irregular, feathered edges of handmade paper.

Felt Used in papermaking to denote the moisture-retentive surface onto which freshly made paper is placed by couching.

Maceration The process that reduces fiber or soaked paper pieces to pulp, e.g., beating or blending.

Mold The frame on which pulp is formed. The mold is a frame with wire mesh stretched over it that fits beneath the deckle.

Pressing The action of using an absorbent material and exerting light pressure on newly formed paper to remove excess moisture.

Pulling The action of moving papermaking frame (deckle and mold held together) downward to bottom of vat filled with paper pulp, flattening paper frame on bottom of vat, and raising paper frame straight up through pulp to just above surface of pulp to allow excess water to drain from deckle.

Pulp The materials used for papermaking in their wet, disintegrated form.

Vat The watertight container used to hold pulp while paper is being pulled.

THE PAPER FRAME

This is the only tool for papermaking that you will need to purchase. Some art-supply stores or paper-making suppliers have readymade frames available. An excellent supplier of readymade frames can be found in the Resource Guide on page 162.

MAKING THE PAPER

Making paper using this method begins with paper to be shredded, soaked, and blended into pulp. The nature of a finished paper depends largely on the papers being used. A general guideline is that the higher the rag content of a pulp, the better it will hold together to make new paper. Pads of watercolor paper—even with water-color drawings—are a good base for pulp. What a good feeling it is to know that all those half-started paintings or sheets of "mistakes" are still useful! The color of a finished paper is also affected by the colors of the papers that make up the pulp. Avoid newspaper, as its high acid content will eventually cause fibers to break down.

A mixture of ¾ watercolor paper to ¼ brown grocery bags will yield a lovely, strong, light-brown paper. Paper can be made entirely of brown-paper bags. It is advisable to make small sheets of this kind, as large sheets will yield a weaker paper that lacks the rag content found in papers of higher quality.

A batch of pulp will yield slightly less paper than the volume of paper being recycled.

MATERIALS:

Six to eight 14x11-inch sheets of 100% rag paper, torn into 2x2-inch pieces

2 brown-paper grocery bags, torn into 2x2-inch pieces

Large bowl

Large square or rectangular dishpan or plastic container

5x8 ½-inch mold and deckle

Blender

Several dish towels for blotting

Large smooth surface

Selection of dried flower petals, herbs, and leaves

Selection of pressed flowers (optional)

To Make the Pulp

STEP 1

To make the pulp, soak the torn paper overnight in a large bowl filled with water.

STEP 2

Place 3 cups water and ½ cup paper pieces in blender. Use chopper blade and blend on high for 45 to 60 seconds. Liquid will become milky-looking. All large paper pieces will be liquefied.

STEP 3

Place 15 cups of water in dishpan. Infusions of herbs or dye plants may be added at this time (see page 97). Add pulp from the blender. Repeat Step 2 four times, adding pulp to dishpan after each batch has been blended. Herbs and petals may be added to the blending process or directly to pulp in dishpan. They will float in pulp and become embedded in paper.

STEP 4

Swirl pulp around in dishpan with hands to suspend it evenly in water.

To Pull a Sheet of Paper

STEP 1

Make a pad of several dish towels and place next to dishpan. Reserve a few towels for blotting.

STEP 2

Place the deckle on top of the mold. Hold pieces together with deckle facing up. Lower into pulp. Move it into a flat position on bottom of dishpan. Use a quick, even motion and bring paper frame straight up. Pulp should cover screen evenly and be approximately ⅛ inch thick. Continue holding deckle in place on mold over dish-pan. Allow excess water to drain from pulp. Pressed flowers, petals, and leaves can be gently pressed into pulp at this stage.

STEP 3

Gently remove deckle from mold. Bring paper to towel pad. Turn mold with paper upside down onto center of towels. Use an extra dishtowel to blot screen to release paper onto towel as well as to remove excess water.

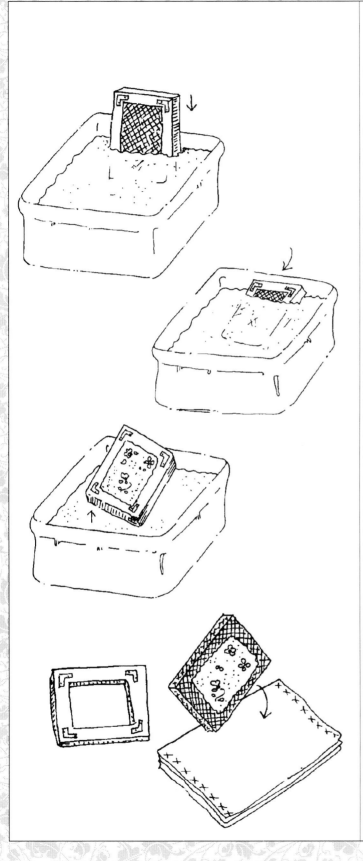

STEP 4

Lift towel with paper sheet and gently turn sheet onto smooth surface to dry. Paper may be blotted again with towel to speed drying process.

Repeat these two processes until all soaked paper bits have been made into pulp and all pulp has been pulled to create paper sheets.

Shaped Paper Projects

It is during Step 3 that paper can be applied to surfaces or shaped. Instead of turning paper sheet onto smooth surface to dry, press from the towel onto wooden boxes or flat-sided baskets. A paper bowl can be formed as well (see page 101). At this wet stage, papers will stick together easily and adhere to surfaces.

Infusions and Dyes

MATERIALS:

1 cup fresh or dried botanicals

2 cups boiling water

1 small bowl

Strainer

STEP 1

Place botanicals in bowl. Pour boiling water over botanicals. Allow to cool. Strain.

STEP 2

Discard herbs. Add infusion to pulp in dishpan. This liquid should be counted as 2 cups of the total liquid poured into the dishpan.

SUGGESTED BOTANICALS FOR INFUSIONS OF COLOR

Bachelor's button, Calendula petals, Lavender, Onion skins, Red poppy petals, Rose madder chips

INFUSIONS FOR SCENT

Lavender, Lemon verbena, Marjoram, Mint, Rosemary, Thyme, Whole cloves

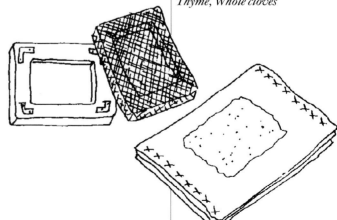

PAPER-COVERED BOX

MATERIALS:

One 4x2x 5-inch-diameter round wooden box with lid

Prepared paper pulp (see page 96)

One 5x5-inch piece of window screen

Several pressed forget-me-nots and leaves

Selection of small pressed petals

14 inches of ⅝-inch hand-dyed teal rayon ribbon

Matte acrylic medium

Round brush

Pencil

Scissors

White craft glue

STEP 1

Place box lid on box and mark around lower rim of box lid with pencil. Remove box top and set aside. Follow instructions on page 96 to make paper sheets. Instead of pulling paper with paper mold and deckle, pull paper using window screen. This sheet of screen will be flexible and allow paper to be pressed around box sides. Press paper around box below pencil line, gently tearing away excess paper along bottom edge of box.

Press paper seams with fingers to smooth. Paper sheet will adhere to box sides. Gently press forget-me-nots and petals into wet paper. Set box aside to allow paper to dry. This will require two to three days.

STEP 2

Repeat Step 1 to cover top surface of box lid with paper and pressed flowers. Allow box top to dry for two to three days.

STEP 3

With brush, apply an even coat of matte medium to top and sides of box. Allow medium to dry before proceeding.

STEP 4

With craft glue, secure ribbon to exterior lip of box lid.

Tip for Coloring Paper With Dyes

Water-based inks and food coloring may be used to dye paper. Add to pulp drop by drop until color becomes pleasing.

WAXED-FLOWERS NOSEGAY

Follow the instructions on page 30 to wax the silica-dried flowers in the Materials list. Wax may be scented with jasmine or rose candle wax to give bouquet a lasting scent.

MATERIALS:

10-12 fuschias

8-10 deep blue delphinium flowers

5-6 small daisies

1 small pink rose

Selection of blue nigella, acacia leaves, and greenery

2 yards of ⅛-inch-wide celery-green antique silk ribbon

Florist's tape

Glue gun/glue sticks

STEP 1

With florist's tape, gently wrap flower stems together. Begin with the rose and add smaller flowers as you tape (see page 42). Smaller flowers with short stems may be secured in place with hot glue. Secure nosegay in cone with hot glue.

STEP 2

Encircle cone with ribbon, beginning at lower back portion and crisscrossing ribbon in front of cone. Secure ribbon in place with dots of hot glue. Cut ribbon ends. Use these ribbon pieces to create streamers glued to front of cone just below nosegay.

HERBAL PAPER NOSEGAY

MATERIALS TO MAKE ONE PAPER CONE:

One 6-inch-square heavy watercolor paper

Stapler

One freshly pulled sheet herbal paper (see page 96)

STEP 1

Make a reusable paper cone from watercolor paper. Wrap paper over onto itself at an angle to form a cone. With stapler, secure top overlap and bottom point.

STEP 2

Following papermaking instructions (see page 96), pull one sheet of paper from pulp. Herbs and flower petals added to pulp will give cone added texture and color.

STEP 3

Instead of placing paper sheet on glass surface to dry, hold towel with fresh paper and wrap around watercolor cone form. Press gently to release fresh paper onto cone shape. Set paper-covered cone on smooth surface to dry.

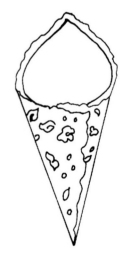

LAVENDER AND ROSEBUD WREATH

MATERIALS:

One 8-inch-diameter straw wreath

2 cups miniature red rosebuds

3 cups dried lavender

1 ½ yards string

White craft glue

Craft brush

6-8 inches craft wire

Glue gun/glue sticks

STEP 1

With hot glue, secure one end of string to wreath back and wind string around wreath base in a spiral fashion, ending at glued end. Secure with hot glue. Trim excess string.

STEP 2

Place wreath on a flat surface and attach a double row of rosebuds along all string lines on front and sides of wreath.

STEP 3

Working in sections with craft glue and brush, coat each section thickly with glue. Pat on lavender to cover. Continue until all areas between rosebuds have been covered. Allow glue to set completely before adding hanger. To attach hanger to wreath back, thread wire through center point on back. Twist ends together to form a loop.

PAPER BOWL

MATERIALS:

One 9-inch-diameter metal bowl

Prepared paper pulp (see page 96)

6x8-inch piece window screen

Selection of flowers and herbs

Spray can of WD-40

Towels and sponges

STEP 1

Prepare paper pulp (see page 96). Invert bowl on a flat, water-resistant surface. Spray outside of bowl with WD-40 or similar mold-release material.

STEP 2

Instead of pulling paper on a paper mold and deckle, use sheet of window screen to pull paper. This screen will be flexible, and freshly pulled paper can be pressed around the curved surfaces of bowl. Repeat process until bowl is covered with several layers of paper.

STEP 3

Gently press flowers and herbs into wet paper surfaces around bowl.

STEP 4

With a towel or sponge, absorb as much water as possible from paper bowl. Drying time will depend upon thickness of paper. Seven to ten days will be required. Gently remove dry paper bowl from metal bowl.

There is always room for tulips. Smooth brown bulbs sleep the winter months away, then pierce the earth to send up great satin cups to green the spring. Explore the world of bulbs this year. Plant the exotic black parrot, a deep, purple-black fringed beauty, among Estella Rynveld.

WAXED TULIP ARRANGEMENT

Information on waxing dried flowers may be found on page 30.

MATERIALS:

One 5 ½-inch terra-cotta flowerpot

One 18-inch freeze-dried lotus leaf

10 silica-dried, waxed magnolia leaves

5 silica-dried, waxed black parrot tulips

6 silica-dried, waxed white tulips

8 silica-dried, waxed Rembrandt tulips

8 silica-dried, waxed fire and ice roses

4 silica-dried, waxed sterling roses

2 generous handfuls sphagnum moss

Oakmoss

Several small, thin twigs

Glue gun/glue sticks

STEP 1

Place lotus leaf in pot and secure leaf to pot edges with hot glue.

STEP 2

With hot glue, secure sphagnum moss to the center of lotus leaf until the hollow area is filled and a mound of approximately 4 inches is obtained. Secure three or four magnolia leaves to base of mound with hot glue.

STEP 3

With hot glue, secure roses and tulips to moss mound, distributing evenly. Secure additional magnolia leaves to moss, distributing evenly. Fill in any gaps with moss.

Looking through the study window to the courtyard garden, where mounds of lavender are buzzing with bees, sweet scents waft in and we are transported to the sister gardens of England. Planting lavender is one of the best ways to achieve drifts of bluish hues in the garden. Add interplantings of Croftway pink, monarda, and delicate, pale-purple Clive Greaves scabious for a gentle, soft color scheme.

PANSY FRAME

MATERIALS:

One 6 ½x5-inch oval wooden frame with glass insert

⅔ yard of 2-inch-wide sky-blue French wired ribbon

Assorted pressed pansies

A few pressed scabious and similar petals

Scissors

Wire cutter

Glue gun/glue sticks

STEP 1

Gather ribbon along both edges (see page 34) until ribbon length will fit around frame exactly. Fold extended wire end of ribbon over on itself ¼ inch. Secure in place with hot glue. With wire cutter, trim excess wire.

STEP 2

Remove frame back and glass insert. With hot glue and working in sections, secure ribbon to both inner and outer edges of frame, covering all wooden surfaces.

STEP 3

Place pansies on ribbon in a pleasing arrangement. Secure in place with dots of hot glue. Glue petals among pansies. Replace glass insert and frame back.

LAVENDER WANDS

MATERIALS:

12-18 long stems fresh lavender

1 yard of ¼-inch-wide antique silk ribbon

STEP 1

Hold lavender stems together with bases of the flowers aligned.

STEP 2

Tie a double knot with ribbon just below flower heads.

STEP 3

Turn stems facing upward, with flower tips facing down. Pull ribbon streamers down through flowers.

STEP 4

Gently bend each flower stem downward to form a cage around flower heads.

STEP 5

Holding stems together, pull ribbon streamers free. Lace ribbons around stems several times. Finish with a small, single bow.

DOLLY SACHETS

MATERIALS FOR GREEN-AND-WHITE-STRIPED SACHET:

One 1 ¼-inch-diameter doll's head

⅓ yard green-striped fabric, cut with pinking or scalloping shears*

25 inches of ³⁄₁₆-inch-wide cream satin ribbon

2 white miniature silk roses, opened

1 cream miniature, silk rose, opened

One ³⁄₄-inch-diameter wooden button

15 preserved boxwood

2 dried feverfew flowers

3 small sprigs purple yarrow

6 sprigs dried yellow statice

One 3-inch piece artificial lily-of-the-valley trim

15 inches of ⁷⁄₁₆-inch-wide white ribbon flower trim

1 ½ cups potpourri

Tracing paper

Pencil

Straight pins

Pinking or scalloping shears

Scissors

Glue gun/glue sticks

*To make a larger sachet doll, increase pattern measurements by 1 inch on all sides.

STEP 1

Using button surface as a base, secure botanical materials to rounded surface with hot glue to create a small bouquet. Set aside.

STEP 2

Using tracing paper and pencil, sachet pattern (see page 107). Cut out traced shape and pin to fabric with stripes running vertically. Cut pattern out of fabric with pinking or scalloping shears. Place fabric on flat surface, right side down, straight side at top. Fold sides inward and overlap edges by ¼ inch. Secure seam with hot glue. With hot glue, secure bottom of fabric. Fill bag with potpourri. Do not overstuff bag.

STEP 3

Place doll's head in open end of bag. Glue fabric around doll's neckline, gathering fabric as you glue. Drape ribbon around neck and crisscross at waist, finishing with a single bow on left front side. Puff fabric where shoulders should be and shake a small amount of potpourri up from bottom of bag. Wrap ribbon securely around waist again and make a small single bow on the left side. Secure ribbon in place with touches of hot glue.

STEP 4

With hot glue, attach trim around bottom and neckline of dress. Add tiny ribbon roses to neckline. Secure lily-of-the-valley trim to doll's head. With hot glue, secure button posy to ribbon at waist.

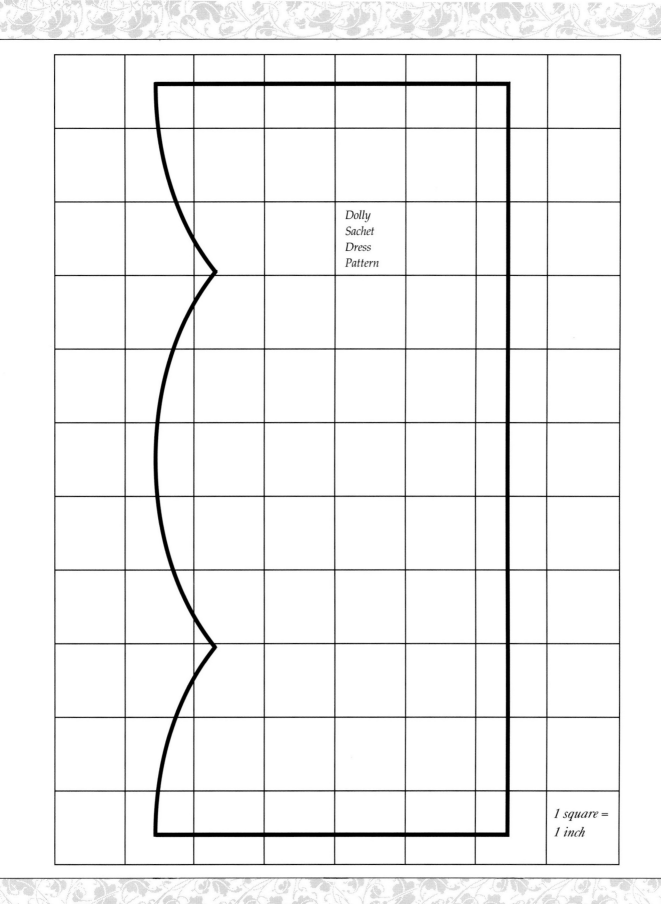

*Dolly
Sachet
Dress
Pattern*

*1 square =
1 inch*

BED GARLAND

MATERIALS:

*4 small silica-dried
sunflowers*

*4 freeze-dried pink or white
medium roses*

2 freeze-dried Candia roses

50 spikes dried lavender

2 freeze-dried pink zinnias

2 freeze-dried violet zinnias

1 dried hollyhock

3 stems dried blue larkspur

2 stems dried pink larkspur

2 dried red cockscombs

3 stems dried statice

2 stems dried sea lavender

*1 bunch small filler flowers
of any variety*

*12 inches ¼-inch-wide
coordinating ribbon*

40 inches of florist's wire

Florist's tape

Wire cutter

Glue gun/glue sticks

STEP 1

Using florist's tape, florist's wire, and a bunch of approximately eight small and filler flowers, tape stems to one wire end (see garland making, page 40). Continue wiring bunches to the wire, adding larger flowers after the third bunch has been wired on. When the halfway point of the wire is reached, begin taping flowers to the other end. Continue working until flowers meet in the center.

STEP 2

Using hot glue, attach a few flowers to center area to fill in any gaps along wire. Garland will be flexible and can be shaped as desired.

STEP 3

To form a hanger, loop ribbon once around top of garland and tie a single bow or knot near ribbon ends.

HYDRANGEA NOSEGAY

MATERIALS:

One 4 ½-inch paper nosegay form

13-15 spikes dried lavender

8 sprigs dried German statice

6 sprigs dried yellow statice

10 sprigs dried pink yarrow

20 sprigs dried ornamental oregano

6 dried hydrangea florets

3 yards of 2-inch-wide luminescent/iridescent green and purple rayon-taffeta ribbon

Seven 3-inch pieces florist's wire

Sharp scissors

Wire cutter

Glue gun/glue sticks

STEP 1

Cut ribbon into seven equal lengths. Form seven double bows with 4-inch streamers (see page 34). Secure bow centers with a twist of florist's wire. Using wire cutter, trim excess wire from each bow. With scissors, trim streamer ends in an inverted V shape. With hot glue, secure bows around the perimeter of the underside of paper nosegay form.

STEP 2

Starting at outer edge of nosegay form, attach spikes of lavender, statice, yarrow, and oregano. Continue gluing stems in concentric circles, distributing flowers and fillers evenly. Secure hydrangea florets at center.

PAINTED PRESSED-FLOWER BOX

MATERIALS:

One 6x3 ½x3-inch wooden recipe box

Light teal and black acrylic paints

Round brush

Fine-line brush

Assorted pressed flowers and leaves (see page 48)

Small piece felt in coordinating color

Scissors

Matte-finish acrylic medium

STEP 1

Trace the bottom of box onto felt. Cut out and glue to bottom of box.

STEP 2

Using round brush, paint entire box with teal paint. Allow paint to dry before proceeding.

STEP 3

Using fine-line brush and acrylic medium, apply medium to the back of a flower and place on box. Medium will act as an adhesive as well as a protective coating. When flower is in place, brush with medium to seal. Continue this process until all botanicals are in place. Pressed flowers and leaves are fairly flexible and can be affixed around box corners to create an overall feeling of painted fabric.

STEP 4

Apply a second coat of acrylic medium over all box surfaces, covering pressed flowers and leaves. Allow varnish to dry completely before proceeding.

STEP 5

Using fine-line brush and black paint, paint around each flower and leaf, allowing a thin band of teal paint to show around botanicals. Allow paint to dry completely before proceeding.

STEP 6

Apply a final coat of acrylic medium to all box surfaces. Allow to dry completely. Additional coats of medium may be added for extra luster. Always allow one coat to dry before adding another.

AUTUMN GARDEN PROJECTS

Days grow shorter, the air is crisp, and the trees drop their first scarlet leaves onto the garden path. Gather the last of the garden blooms

Ah, Sunflowers, weary of Time, Who countest the steps of the sun; Seeking after that sweet golden clime Where the traveller's journey is done;...

WILLIAM BLAKE, 1757–1827

WREATH OF SUNFLOWERS

MATERIALS:

One 8-inch-diameter wreath of sweet annie

5 silica-dried sunflowers

2-3 freeze-dried whole oranges

2-3 dried whole pomegranates

7-8 dried slices orange, 2 cut in half

3 slices dried squash

6 small dried kumquats or tiny mandarin oranges

7 small bunches dried yarrow

8 small bunches dried artemisia florets

Three 12-inch pieces florist's wire

Glue gun/glue sticks

STEP 1

With glue gun, secure sunflowers to wreath, distributing flowers evenly. Attach whole oranges and pomegranates to front of wreath with hot glue. Glue orange and squash slices among flowers and fruits on wreath. Fill in gaps with yarrow, mandarin oranges, and artemisia florets.

STEP 2

To form hanger, push one end of florist's wire through the back top center point of wreath base. Twist ends together to form a loop. To create a double sunflower wreath, make a second wreath and wind florist's wire around wire wreath base at bottom of first wreath. Thread other end through hanger of second wreath.

Fields of bright sunflowers, their faces following the golden light, look, from a distance, like yellow paint poured upon the earth. Plant a circle of sunflowers and place a bench in the center. You will soon have a room for thinking happy thoughts.

CITRUS FRUIT POMANDER

MATERIALS FOR ONE POMANDER:

1 fresh orange, lemon, or lime

1 cup whole cloves

1 tablespoon orrisroot

1 tablespoon ground cinnamon

1 ½ teaspoons ground cloves

Small crockery bowl

Push pointed ends of cloves into citrus fruit's peel. Arrange cloves in patterns or stripes. Color of peel should show in between clove patterns. Set aside. Mix remaining materials in bowl and roll the clove-studded fruit in mixture. Makes several citrus pomanders to display in a basket or bowl to impart a spicy scent to rooms.

SUNFLOWER BASKET

MATERIALS:

One 9x7x4-inch sweet annie basket with tall handle

2-3 small dried sunflowers

4 slices dried orange, cut in half

6 small slices dried orange

2 whole nutmegs

2 dried cedar roses

1 dried pod

Small amount dried gold yarrow

Small amount dried white yarrow

Small amount dried acacia

Glue gun/glue sticks

At the base of one handle, secure largest sunflower in place with hot glue. Attach remaining flowers and fruit in a pleasing pattern around main sunflower. Use yarrow, acacia, cedar roses, pod, and nutmegs to fill in any gaps.

SUNFLOWER POTPOURRI

MATERIALS:

4 cups loosely packed dried sunflower petals

2 cups dried calendula petals

2 cups dried tansy flowers

2 cups dried golden yarrow pieces

2 cups dried bay leaves

2 cups sweet annie sprigs

1 cup star anise

14 quarters dried orange slices

10 broken cinnamon sticks

1 cup juniper berries

1 cup rosehips

Large handful oakmoss cut into small pieces

6 tablespoons orrisroot

8 drops lemon oil

4 drops chamomile oil

2 drops rosemary oil

To make potpourri, see instructions on page 44.

Sunflowers were once worshiped in the Inca culture as the symbol of the sun.
—FOLKLORE

Rosemary, sweet marjoram, and thyme grow carelessly along the pathway. Herbs may be collected long after the flowers of the garden have gone. Clippings of herbs may be used as a simmer to recall the scents of summer one last time...

SAMPLER WREATH

MATERIALS:

One 16-inch-diameter twig wreath base

12 small bunches yellow yarrow

17 orange strawflowers

20 dried deep red roses

50 spikes dried lavender

1 bunch dried white feverfew

1 handful reindeer or Spanish moss

1 bunch blue statice

1 bunch allium seed heads

1 generous handful dried rose leaves

12 inches twine

Glue gun/glue sticks

STEP 1

With hot glue, attach each botanical material to wreath in a tight grouping to create blocks of color and texture.

STEP 2

To form hanger, thread twine through twigs and knot at top to form loop.

Fondest memories of winters passed in the homey kitchen of an old friend, having coffee while cinnamon buns cool a bit. The birds hover around a snowy bird feeder, and the talk turns to next year's garden...

APPLESAUCE CINNAMON BIRDS

This mixture produces a highly scented, non-edible dough that can be rolled and cut with cookie cutters. The mixture can also be rolled into balls by hand. Cutout shapes are delicate and require careful handling.

MATERIALS:

1 ½ cups cinnamon

1 cup applesauce

Extra cinnamon

Waxed paper

Rolling pin

Small and medium bird-shaped cookie cutters

Metal spatula

Toothpick or nail

Bowl

Spoon

Plastic bag

STEP 1

In bowl mix applesauce with 1 ½ cups cinnamon. Press together by hand until materials hold together well. Place dough ball in plastic and allow to sit at room temperature for two to three hours. Sprinkle extra cinnamon on waxed paper. Remove dough from plastic bag. Knead dough between hands for several minutes. Place a handful of dough on extra cinnamon. Sprinkle more cinnamon on dough and place a second sheet of waxed paper on top.

STEP 2

With rolling pin, gently roll dough out to a thickness of approximately ¼ inch. Remove top sheet of waxed paper. Use cookie cutters to cut out bird shapes. Remove excess dough from around shapes. Pat edges gently with the back of a spoon to smooth any irregular edges. Use toothpick or nail and pierce the top surface to add dotted outline of wings. To make eye, pierce a hole all the way through dough. Allow shapes to air-dry completely in a warm place for three to four days.

CINNAMON BIRD WREATH

MATERIALS:

6 small cinnamon-bird ornaments

2 medium cinnamon-bird ornaments

One 10-inch twig wreath base

1 bunch lavender leaves

1 bunch silver santolina

1 bunch silver artemisia

1 bunch dusty-miller leaves

Eight to ten 4-inch pussy willow tips

24-26 white globe amaranth

12-14 large rosehips

8 inches of ¼-inch-wide green ribbon

Glue gun/glue sticks

STEP 1

Make Applesauce Cinnamon recipe. Cut out two large birds and six small birds. Make extras as they are delicate and could break.

STEP 2

Use hot glue to attach lavender, santolina, artemisia, and dusty miller around the front of wreath. Distribute botanicals evenly.

STEP 3

Cut all botanical stems into 4-inch sprigs. Use hot glue to attach birds to wreath. Glue the two large birds near the bottom and one small bird in between them. Secure the remaining five small birds at the top and sides.

STEP 4

With hot glue, secure rosehips and globe amaranth among silver foliage.

STEP 5

To create a hanger, thread ribbon through twigs on the back of wreath and tie ends together to form a loop.

CINNAMON BIRD MATERIALS:

One 2x4x4 ½-inch oval bark basket with rounded top

1 piece plastic foam cut to fit basket

Oakmoss

1 large Applesauce Cinnamon bird shape

15-20 melaleuca or bay leaves

8-10 large rosehips

Few sprigs silver santolina

One 5-inch piece florist's wire

Glue gun/glue sticks

STEP 1

With hot glue, secure plastic foam in basket. Cover domed surface completely with moss and secure in place with hot glue.

STEP 2

Push florist's wire into foam center. Allow it to protrude 3 inches. This will act as a brace for the bird. With hot glue, secure bird in place in front of wire brace.

STEP 3

With hot glue, attach leaves and rosehips around bird, distributing evenly. Secure sprigs of santolina around base of bird with hot glue.

Make a round Applesauce Cinnamon ball and decorate it with berries and greenery. Hang in cupboards for a spicy scent.

BOTANICAL PLATE

Design your own set of botanical plates for a wall display. Wrapping papers, prints, greeting cards, and even photographs may be used to create decorative plates. Clear-glass plates are usually available at kitchen shops and some import stores. Decorated plates are not dishwasher-safe, but they can be cleaned by wiping with a damp cloth.

MATERIALS:

One 8-inch-diameter clear-glass plate

1 paper cutout of yellow iris (or other flower of choice)

Acrylic gloss medium

Round brush

Maroon acrylic paint (or other color of choice)

Sheet of white paper

STEP 1

Place sheet of white paper on flat work surface. Turn plate upside down on center of paper. Using brush, apply an even coat of gloss medium to front of paper flower. Place flower onto center of plate. Smooth paper to secure and eliminate air bubbles. Allow gloss medium to dry for approximately 20 minutes.

STEP 2

Apply an even coat of gloss medium to entire back of plate. Cover wrong side of paper flower as well. Allow approximately 20 minutes for gloss medium to dry.

STEP 3

With round brush, apply an even coat of paint to entire back of plate. Allow paint to dry completely before proceeding. Apply a second coat of paint. Allow paint to dry completely before proceeding.

STEP 4

Apply a final coat of gloss medium to painted surface. Allow approximately 20 minutes for gloss medium to dry.

Use the predominant colors in fabrics chosen for doll's clothing to paint a doll's chair for your display. Apply two coats of acrylic paint for complete coverage. Allow paint to dry completely between coats.

GARDEN DOLL

MATERIALS:

1 package air-dry white craft clay

One 13-inch plastic foam cone

One 20x20-inch provincial-print hemmed cloth napkin

⅛ yard red floral-print fabric

¼ yard mustard-yellow floral-print fabric

Cotton batting

¾ yard of ¼-inch-wide navy-blue antique silk ribbon

¾ yard of ½-inch-wide navy-blue French wired ribbon

Fifteen 12-inch pieces raffia-type garden twine for hair

One 5-inch-diameter straw doll's hat

White, brown, blue, and red acrylic paint

Round brush

Fine-line brush

Pencil

Scissors

Pinking or scalloping shears

Liquid fray retardant

Glue gun/glue sticks

STEP 1

With the clay, make one head-and-shoulders piece. Head can be formed by rolling some between hands to form a slightly egg-shaped ball. Neck shape is a cylinder approximately 3 ½ inches around and 1 inch tall.

Smooth neck to head to join pieces. Shoulders are approximately 1 inch deep. Attach neck to shoulders and smooth over. Set aside to air-dry. Form two hand-and-wrist sections. Set aside to air-dry. Follow manufacturer's suggested drying time.

STEP 2

With round brush, mix dots of brown and red paint with 1 tablespoon of white paint until desired skin color is achieved. For dolls with darker skin tones, add more brown paint with a deeper red mixed for cheeks and lips. Paint head, neck, hands, and wrists. Leave shoulders unpainted. Allow paint to dry completely before proceeding.

STEP 3

With fine-line brush and color of choice, paint facial details on head. If a mistake occurs, allow paint to dry and repaint with skin color. Use face drawing as a guide only; each doll will be slightly different. Paint nose and eyebrows first in order to better place eyes and mouth. Paint interior of eye area white. Add desired eye color after white paint dries. Add a tiny dot of white paint to irises to add more life to the eyes. Allow paint to dry completely before proceeding.

STEP 4

With scissors, cut napkin to yield two sleeves and one dress body. Cut mustard-yellow fabric to make one apron body. Cut one 1x28-inch strip of mustard fabric for apron waistband.

Cut red fabric to make one pocket. Cut one ½-inch strip of red fabric for skirt trim. Cut two red floral strips 1 ¾x3 inches for wristbands, pinking one of the longer edges. Treat all raw edges with liquid fray retardant. Allow to dry according to manufacturer's instructions.

STEP 5

Place center indentation on top of cone. With hot glue, attach doll shoulders to top of plastic foam cone.

STEP 6

Place one sleeve piece on a flat surface right side down. Fold sides to meet and overlap by ½ inch. Secure seam with hot glue. Glue one end of sleeve over wrist area of hand piece. Gather as needed. Use pencil to gently stuff batting into sleeve. Leave 1 inch unstuffed at open end. With hot glue, attach one 3-inch strip of red floral print around wrist to create cuff. Repeat process for second sleeve. With hot glue, attach arms to shoulders.

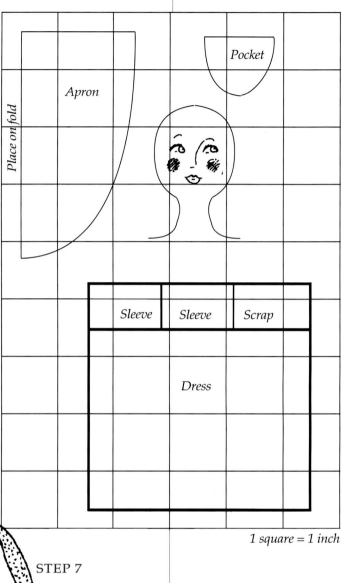

1 square = 1 inch

STEP 7

Place dress body piece on flat surface, right side up, raw edge toward the top. Glue 1x21-inch strip of red fabric to lower edge of dress piece 1 inch from hemline. Turn piece over. Fold sides inward to meet and overlap 1 inch. Secure with hot glue to form back seam. Fold top raw edge over 1 inch and secure with hot glue. Place dress over cone with red band at bottom. Working in sections and gathering as needed, glue top edge to shoulders. Allow arms to protrude.

STEP 8

Center apron waistband on apron body piece. With hot glue, fasten both pieces together, gathering apron body slightly. Glue red pocket piece to left-hand side of apron. Tie apron around doll body. Finish with a simple bow.

STEP 9

Use ¼-inch-wide navy ribbon to encircle doll's waist several times. Finish with a simple bow. Cut one 12-inch piece of twine into 2-inch pieces. Set aside. With hot glue, secure 12-inch pieces of twine to doll's head for hair. Attach 2-inch pieces to forehead to create bangs. Separate twine to create feathery, strawlike hair.

STEP 10

Use ½-inch-wide navy ribbon to tie a hatband around straw hat. Finish in a double bow with long streamers (see page 34). Secure in place with hot glue.

STEP 11

Make little arrangements and baskets filled with dried flowers and herbs for the Garden Doll to hold.

Adapt this doll to represent a special gardener in your life. Substitute doll hair from the craft shop in the color of your choice.

To make small arrangements for the Garden Doll, gather tiny sprigs of flowers, small leaves, and bits of moss. Using spray adhesive, secure scraps of fabric around tiny flowerpots and attach florist's foam, moss, and flowers with hot glue. Small baskets and clay pots make delightful little arrangements as well.

Moisten a small paper doily to wrap around a bunch of tiny flowers for doll to hold. Paper doily will be pliable when moist and should wrap easily around flowers.

MINIATURE COVERED FLOWERPOT

MATERIALS:

One 2x1 1/2-inch-diameter terra-cotta flowerpot

2 1/2x6-inch scrap of provincial-print fabric

Sphagnum moss

Several dried fern sprigs

Spray adhesive

Glue gun/glue sticks

STEP 1

Cover wrong side of fabric with spray adhesive. Smooth fabric around flowerpot. Tuck edges inside pot and under bottom. Place sphagnum moss inside flowerpot. With hot glue, secure ferns to moss.

MINIATURE BIRDHOUSE

MATERIALS:

One 2 1/2x1 1/2x1 1/2-inch wooden birdhouse ornament

6-inch square of floral wrapping paper

Three 1-inch plastic birds

Small amount oakmoss

Small craft knife

White craft glue

Glue gun/glue sticks

Wrap birdhouse in paper and secure with craft glue. With craft knife, trim paper around hole, bird perch, and under roof. With hot glue, secure oakmoss thickly to roof. With hot glue, attach one bird to perch, two birds to rooftop.

TINY HEATHER TOPIARY

MATERIALS:

One 1 1/4x1 1/4-inch-diameter terra-cotta flowerpot

Oakmoss

Several sprigs dried heather

Glue gun/glue sticks

Place oakmoss in flowerpot. With hot glue, secure sprigs of heather to moss.

MOSSY ROSEBUD WREATH

MATERIALS:

11 inches craft wire

Small amount sphagnum

25 baby rosebuds in assorted colors

6 spikes dried lavender

Selection of small dried pink flowers

5 sprigs dried baby's breath

Glue gun/glue sticks

STEP 1

Form a 3-inch-diameter circle of craft wire and twist ends around each other to secure. With hot glue, secure oakmoss to wire to form wreath base.

STEP 2

With hot glue, secure all flowers to wreath base.

MINIATURE FLOWER BASKETS

MATERIALS FOR ONE BASKET:

One small wicker basket

3 spikes dried lavender

7 cockscombs

Selection of small flowers and filler plant materials

Glue gun/glue sticks

With hot glue, secure all flowers into basket in a random but pleasing arrangement.

Autumn apples scent the shed, bringing the remembrance of times past...putting the apple butter by in the fruit cellar with Grandmother. The time has come to plan projects for flowers gathered and dried during the summer months.

KITCHEN GARLAND

MATERIALS:

One 36-inch natural raffia braid with top loop

Generous handful dried bay leaves

4 bulbs large white garlic

4 bulbs small purple garlic

10 small yellow onions

6 small purple onions

50-60 dried red chili peppers

Glue gun/glue sticks

STEP 1

With hot glue, attach a base of bay leaves to raffia braid so that the leaf points are slanted out and down. Attach stems of garlic and onions, evenly distributed among the leaves, in a pleasing pattern until garland front and sides are covered.

STEP 2

Fill in gaps with dried chili peppers and a few small bay leaves.

SWEET ANNIE AND PEPPERBERRY WREATH

MATERIALS:

One 12-inch sweet annie wreath

20 sprigs red pepperberries

12 slices dried lemons

9 nigella seedpods

40-45 spikes dried lavender

12 lion's tail

14 sprigs dried dusty-miller flowers

30-35 dried melaleuca or bay leaves

Glue gun/glue sticks

With hot glue, follow the direction of the sweet annie and secure pepperberries, nigella, lemon slices, and lion's tail in place, distributing evenly. Fill in gaps with leaves, dusty miller, and lavender spikes.

Long walks in the country yield acorns and leaves, mossy twigs, and gray-green lichen for autumn crafting. Parting with summer days is somehow easier with a pocketful of little treasures and a warm fire waiting at home.

AUTUMN GARLAND

MATERIALS:

One 3-foot sweet annie garland

3 yards 3-inch-wide gold organdy ribbon

3 yards 3-inch-wide pale turquoise organdy ribbon

4 yards 1 ½-inch-wide deep green organdy ribbon

7 dried pomegranates

24 nigella pods

15 seedpods

9 small freeze-dried oranges

15 sprigs dill

Glue gun/glue sticks

STEP 1

With hot glue, secure all pods to garland, distributing evenly.

STEP 2

With hot glue, attach oranges and pomegranates, distributing evenly. Fill in any gaps with dill sprigs.

STEP 3

Wind the ribbons through the spray and use hot glue to secure in place.

ACORN NOSEGAY

MATERIALS:

One 3-inch-diameter paper nosegay form

11 dried bay leaves

Small amount sweet annie

Small amount dried dock

18 sprays flaxseed pods

4 small acorns

1 large acorn

Cinnamon essential oil

Glue gun/glue sticks

STEP 1

With hot glue, secure bay leaves to paper form. Secure large acorn, stem down, to center of form. Attach sweet annie, dried dock, and flaxseed pods to bay leaves around the acorn.

STEP 2

Secure the small acorns, evenly distributed, among other materials. Add a few drops of cinnamon oil to the center acorn cap.

AUTUMN CANDLES

MATERIALS FOR ONE CANDLESTICK:

One 8 ½-inch turquoise metal candlestick

16 inches of aluminum bonsai wire

Handful Spanish moss

2 sprigs sweet annie

2 sprigs baby's breath

2 slices dried orange peel, broken into 4 pieces

1 slice dried squash, broken into 3 pieces

2-3 nigella seedpods

1 small dried mandarin orange or artificial pumpkin

STEP 1

Use hot glue to secure moss around entire length of wire. Twist mossed wire tightly around candlestick, beginning at upper left and ending at lower right side. Allow 2 to 3 inches to extend beyond the candlestick at each end.

STEP 2

With hot glue, attach sweet annie to moss. Attach remaining botanicals to moss in a pleasing arrangement.

WINTER GARDEN PROJECTS

The most sensitive of plants is surely the fern, nestled beneath the trees, shrinking from the midday sun, happiest with a light morning mist. These gardens of green grace the forest floor, each fern delighting in the ever-shifting patterns of light.

MAIDENHAIR FERN WREATH

The ferns for this wreath were purchased, as bleaching botanicals is a commercial process. A source for these ferns is listed in the Resource Guide on page 162. Preserved green ferns may be substituted for a more traditional green and red wreath. Substitute a red silk ribbon on a green wreath.

MATERIALS:

One 14-inch bleached willow wreath base

3 bunches glycerin-preserved bleached maidenhair fern

1 bunch red pepperberries with leaves

1 bunch glycerin-preserved miniature baby's breath

2 ½ yards of 4 ½-inch-wide moss-green French wired ribbon

2-4 inches florist's wire

Wire cutter

Glue gun/glue sticks

STEP 1

Separate ferns into 6-8-inch-long stems. Work on a flat surface and attach ferns to wreath base with hot glue (see page 39).

STEP 2

Divide pepperberry bunches into four equal amounts and secure to wreath with hot glue. Space bunches evenly.

STEP 3

Glue sprigs of baby's breath, evenly distributed, throughout wreath.

STEP 4

Cut one 28-inch and one 8-inch piece of ribbon. Set aside. Use remaining ribbon to form a single bow gathered along both edges (see page 34). Secure center with a twist of florist's wire. Use wire cutter to trim ends. With 8-inch ribbon piece, form a double-gathered bow center (see page 34).

Glue ends together at back of bow to secure. Set bow aside. Hold remaining ribbon at center point and twist florist's wire around center point. Finish each ribbon end in an inverted V shape. Glue this streamer to wreath, centered between two pepperberry groupings. Glue bow to center of streamer piece. Drape streamer and tuck into ferns.

Snowflakes fall and the holly berries are red and ripe. Candles glow in windows frosted with patterns on a winter's night. Joyful voices of carolers echo over the icy blue snow, kindling in us the spirit of Christmas.

CHRISTMAS TOPIARY

This project has a special secret. The beautiful urn used for this elegant topiary was created from recycled metal—a very special Christmas gift to our environment, indeed. The supplier for this urn can be found in the Resource Guide on page 162.

MATERIALS:

One 2-foot-high plastic foam cone

1 large iron urn or similar container

Plastic foam cut to fit container

Sphagnum moss

2 1/3 yards of 3 1/2-inch-wide deep burgundy French wired ribbon

2 yards small wired gold beads

2 yards of 1/4-inch-wide gold cording

2 yards aluminum bonsai wire

One 4-inch gold wire star

Tacky glue

Glue gun/glue sticks

STEP 1

Use hot glue to cover entire cone with moss.

STEP 2

Allowing 2 inches of wire to remain exposed at each end, wrap ribbon around wire. Overlap ribbon so all wire areas are covered. Secure ribbon with touches of hot glue. Wrap wired gold beads around ribbon and secure with hot glue. Wrap gold cord around gold beads, securing in place with hot glue.

STEP 3

Attach the wire at the top by forcing it into the plastic foam cone. Circle the tree in a spiral fashion, allowing spiral approximately 1 inch free space between tree and wrapped wire. Attach wire at the bottom by forcing it into the cone. Place wire star on top of topiary.

STEP 4

With hot glue, secure foam cut to fit container in container. Secure topiary to foam in pot using hot glue.

ROUND SACHET PILLOW

MATERIALS:

28 inches of 4 1/4-inch-wide green French wired ribbon

30 inches of 4 1/4-inch wide burgundy French wired ribbon

One 1-inch-diameter covered button blank

Potpourri

Cotton batting

Green and burgundy thread and needle

Wire cutter

Scissors

Glue gun/ glue sticks

STEP 1

Use scissors to cut a 2-inch piece of burgundy ribbon. Cover button blank with ribbon piece, following button cover manufacturer's instructions. Set button aside.

STEP 2

Use remaining burgundy ribbon piece and gather ribbon tightly along one wire edge (see page 33). Secure both ends of ruffled ribbon folds with hot glue. Sew ribbon ends together to form a seam. Set piece aside.

STEP 3

Gather green ribbon tightly along wire edge (see page 33). Secure both ends of ruffled ribbon folds with hot glue. Sew ribbon ends together to form a seam. Stitch green ribbon to burgundy ribbon 1/4 inch from edge. Leave a 2-inch opening at bottom of circle shape. Center point of pillow will be tightly gathered on both sides. Do not turn pillow right side out.

STEP 4

Stuff pillow with potpourri and batting. Stitch opening closed.

STEP 5

Use hot glue to fasten covered button to center of green side of pillow.

DECORATIVE SANTA PLATE

Clear-glass plates can be decoupaged on the back to create decorative accent pieces for display with projects of natural materials. Use Victorian paper scraps or wrapping-paper images to decorate your plate. This plate is not dishwasher-safe and is for decorative purposes only. Clean surface by wiping with a damp cloth.

MATERIALS:

One 5-inch clear-glass saucer

Christmas wrapping paper with Santa motif

1 sheet white paper

Deep green acrylic paint

Metallic gold acrylic paint

Deep red acrylic paint

Acrylic gloss medium

Round brush

Scissors

STEP 1

Cut out Santa face. Place saucer upside down on white paper. Using brush, apply an even coat of gloss medium to right side of Santa face. Position paper facedown on center of saucer. Smooth out any air bubbles under paper piece. Allow medium to dry for approximately 20 minutes before proceeding.

STEP 2

Apply an even coat of gloss medium to entire back of saucer, covering paper as well as glass surface. Allow medium to dry for approximately 20 minutes before proceeding.

STEP 3

Paint a halo of metallic gold paint around Santa piece. Allow paint to dry before proceeding. Apply an even coat of green paint to entire back of saucer, covering paper piece with paint. Allow paint to dry completely and apply a second even coat of green paint. Allow paint to dry completely before proceeding.

STEP 4

Apply a final coat of gloss medium to entire back of saucer. Allow medium to dry for approximately 20 minutes.

STEP 5

Turn saucer right side up. Using brush, apply an even coat of red paint around rim. Allow paint to dry completely before proceeding. Apply a second coat of red paint. Allow paint to dry. Apply an even coat of gloss medium to rim. Allow at least 20 minutes for gloss medium to set before handling saucer.

GREEN-ON-GREEN FABRIC WREATH

MATERIALS:

One 7-inch-diameter straw wreath

4x50-inch strip of green-on-green-striped material

Six 2-inch twigs

12 sprigs greenery

Small amount reindeer moss

Six 1-inch pinecones

9 sprigs red pepperberries

Six 4-inch pieces of 1 ½-inch-wide red-and-green-striped, gold-edged French wired ribbon

Scissors

Glue gun/glue sticks

STEP 1

With hot glue, attach one edge of fabric strip to back of wreath. Wrap fabric around wreath at an angle until entire wreath has been covered. Secure remaining edge to back of wreath with hot glue. Trim excess fabric.

STEP 2

With hot glue, secure twigs and greenery to top of wreath. Attach moss, pinecones, and pepperberries to greenery and twigs. Form ribbon pieces into single loops and secure to wreath with hot glue. Ribbons may be attached behind or to the greenery and berries.

WHITE & GREEN FABRIC WREATH

MATERIALS:

One 6-inch straw wreath

4x50-inch strip of green-and-white-striped fabric, gold edging around the green stripe

16 small sprigs preserved boxwood

Six 2-inch twigs

Six 2-inch cinnamon sticks

5 dried red globe amaranth

4 whole nutmegs

4 rosehips

4 small cones

Scissors

Glue gun/glue sticks

STEP 1

With hot glue, attach one edge of fabric strip to back of wreath. Wrap fabric around wreath at an angle until entire wreath has been covered. Secure remaining edge to back of wreath with hot glue. Trim excess fabric.

STEP 2

With hot glue, secure twigs and leaves to wreath. Attach moss and nuts to twigs and leaves. Add nuts and amaranth and secure in place with hot glue. Attach cinnamon sticks at an angle around nuts and amaranth. With hot glue, attach four cones to center of natural materials. Secure rosehips around cones.

Celebrate Christmas at home this year. The wreath on the door heralds the warmth and good cheer within. Light many candles and bake cookies for chilly-night snacks. Let us relish this feeling all through the coming year.

CHRISTMAS CANDLES

MATERIALS FOR ONE CANDLE:

1 glass votive candle holder

8 inches ¹/₂-inch-wide red and gold organdy or satin ribbon

Three ¹/₄-inch pieces cinnamon stick

2 miniature pinecones

1 sprig red pepperberries

Three 1-inch sprigs preserved cedar

Spanish moss

Glue gun/glue sticks

1 white votive candle

STEP 1

With hot glue, secure moss to sides and bottom of glass votive candle holder. Encircle candle holder with ribbon, knotting in center.

STEP 2

With hot glue, attach cinnamon sticks and pinecones to ribbon at knot. Fill in any gaps with bits of cedar. With hot glue, add a sprig of pepperberries to center. Place votive candle in holder.

SANTA AND TOY PLATE

Christmas fabrics, cut to fit plate back, are perfect backgrounds for cutout paper pieces.

This plate is not dishwasher-safe. Clean surface by wiping with a damp cloth.

MATERIALS:

One 7-inch clear-glass dessert plate

1 circle green-and-red-print fabric, cut to fit back of plate

Christmas wrapping paper with Santa and toy motifs

1 sheet white paper

Deep red acrylic paint

Acrylic gloss medium

Round brush

Scissors

STEP 1

Cut out Santa and selection of toys and Christmas motifs from wrapping paper. Set aside.

STEP 2

Place plate upside down on white paper. Using brush, apply an even coat of gloss medium to right side of Santa piece. Position face down on center of plate.

STEP 3

Smooth paper to eliminate any air bubbles. Repeat procedure with small cutouts, placing them around plate border, evenly spaced. Allow approximately 20 minutes for gloss medium to set before proceeding.

STEP 4

Apply an even coat of gloss medium to entire back of plate. Cover the backs of paper pieces. Place fabric circle, print side down, on plate. Smooth to eliminate air bubbles. Smoothing from the center outward will push any air pockets outward toward rim of plate. Allow medium to set before proceeding.

STEP 5

Apply an even coat of medium over fabric surface to seal. Allow medium to set before proceeding.

STEP 6

Turn plate right side up. Using brush, apply an even coat of red paint around rim. Allow paint to dry completely before proceeding. Apply a second coat of red paint. Allow paint to dry. Apply an even coat of gloss medium to rim. Allow at least 20 minutes for gloss medium to set before handling plate.

CHRISTMAS TABLE ARRANGEMENT

Days are shorter and there is more time for candlelight. Savor the stillness of twilight hours, and experience the quiet in this room, so specially dressed for the holidays.

MATERIALS:

One 3 1/2x4-inch-diameter terra-cotta pot

One 4 1/2x5-inch-diameter terra-cotta pot

One 5 1/2x6-inch-diameter terra-cotta pot

1 1/2 yards red floral provincial-print border fabric

Plastic foam cut to fit all three pots

1 bunch preserved cedar

1 stem preserved pine

4-6 stems dried sea lavender

10-12 sprigs assorted greens and twigs

25-28 artificial raspberries

15-17 small bunches acorns, varying sizes

20-25 small red Christmas ornaments

Sphagnum moss

Sharp scissors

Spray adhesive

Fabric pen

Measuring tape

Glue gun/glue sticks

STEP 1

Using tape measure, measure around flat pot-rim area. Add 1 inch for fabric overlap. Measure the depth of the rim. Add 1 inch to this measurement. Mark fabric with fabric pen and cut out. Use spray adhesive applied to wrong side of fabric strip. Center fabric around pot rim. Smooth 1/2 inch over and into pot interior. Smooth 1/2 inch below rim.

STEP 2

Measure circumference of pot below rim and depth. Using these measurements, make a rectangle on fabric with fabric marker. Cut out. As lower sections of pots are graduated in size, fabric will have to be trimmed to fit shape exactly. Wrap fabric around pot area to be covered. Using fabric pen, mark cloth and cut out shape. Cover wrong side of fabric with spray adhesive. Smooth cloth around pot to cover. Should any gaps occur, use fabric scraps to piece. Repeat Steps 1 and 2 for remaining pots.

STEP 3

Place plastic foam in all pot interiors. Secure in place with hot glue. Place medium pot on top of largest pot and press into plastic foam. Secure in place with hot glue. Place smaller pot into medium and press into plastic foam. Secure in place with hot glue.

STEP 4

Arrange greenery in pots and secure in place with hot glue. Intersperse flowers and other botanicals. Add acorns, ornaments, and raspberries to create a full arrangement.

RASPBERRY BASKET

MATERIALS:

One 8x6x4-inch oval wicker basket with handle

Hunter-green and brick-red acrylic paint

Round brush

20 artificial raspberries

Handful preserved boxwood

Glue gun/glue sticks

STEP 1

With brush and red paint, paint basket body. Allow paint to dry before proceeding. With brush and hunter-green paint, paint basket rim and handle. Allow paint to dry before proceeding.

STEP 2

With hot glue, attach boxwood leaves around rim of basket. Attach leaves in a spray below each handle. With hot glue, secure raspberries to leaves, distributing evenly. Place three raspberries in leaf spray below each handle.

MERRY CHRISTMAS NOSEGAY

MATERIALS:

One 4-inch paper nosegay holder

9 silk rose leaves

1 branch cedar

Handful preserved boxwood leaves

1 white strawflower

9 artificial red berries

3 red globe amaranth

Glue gun/glue sticks

STEP 1

Use hot glue to attach silk leaves around perimeter of nosegay holder.

STEP 2

With hot glue, secure a ring of 2-inch cedar sprigs around holder. Glue cedar sprigs on top of leaves with glue placed on base of leaves. Secure boxwood leaves in a ring on top of cedar sprigs.

STEP 3

With hot glue, attach strawflower to center. Glue berries and globe amaranth around flower, placing berries in groups of three and globe amaranth between berry clusters.

APPLES AND IVY CHRISTMAS WREATH

Garnet pomegranates nestled in boughs of pine grace the holiday table. Christmas traditions old and new are brought together during this season of giving. Create your own tradition by crafting special decorations with unusual materials.

Fresh ivy can be woven in and around twigs to create wreaths of green and variegated leaves. Ivy will dry in place. Keep dried ivy away from direct sunlight to preserve leaf color and shape.

MATERIALS:

One 18-inch twig wreath base

Five or six 16-inch fresh ivy stems

Twelve to fifteen 8-inch fresh rosemary stems

Eight to ten 5-inch stems preserved boxwood

1 bunch preserved cedar

20 large dried apple slices

1 ½ yards 1-inch-wide green-red-and-white tartan ribbon

One 4-inch piece florist's wire

One 8-inch piece florist's wire

3 pine-green metal bells

Glue gun/glue sticks

STEP 1

Twine fresh ivy stems through twigs on wreath front. Leave top right-hand quarter of circle open except for one ivy strand. Use hot glue to secure stems in place if necessary.

STEP 2

Create a crescent-shaped floral area on wreath front by gluing cedar sprigs, rosemary stems, and boxwood pieces to wreath. Allow upper-right quarter of twigs on wreath to remain exposed. Distribute materials evenly. Allow tips of stems and leaves to overlap wreath edges.

STEP 3

With hot glue, attach apple slices among the botanical materials.

STEP 4

Form a six-loop bow 7 inches wide overall, with 12-inch streamers (see page 34). Secure bow center with 4-inch piece florist's wire. Finish streamer ends in an inverted V shape. With hot glue, secure bow to lower left side of wreath. Drape streamers in greenery and secure in place with dots of hot glue.

STEP 5

Use remaining wire to form a hanger. Thread through twigs at top center point on back of wreath. Twist ends together.

WINTER FRUIT CANDLESTICK

The two-part, spiked candle holder, often used to transform fresh pineapple into beautiful centerpieces during the holidays, is useful for all manner of table arrangements. Candle base and cup can be spaced with a block of water-saturated florist's foam covered with fresh flowers. A supplier for this candle base and cup is listed in the Resource Guide on page 162.

MATERIALS:

One 2-piece dark-green metal spiked candle cup with metal base

One 5x3-inch rectangle florist's foam

6 dried whole pomegranates

23 dried apple slices

Small handful red pepperberries

35 dried melaleuca or bay leaves

Handful lichen

Candle

Glue gun/glue sticks

STEP 1

Mount oasis rectangle onto candlestick spike. With hot glue, attach a few apple slices around green metal leaves of candlestick base. Add a few sprigs of pepperberries and leaves.

STEP 2

With hot glue, begin second layer, adding whole pome-granates, pepperberries, leaves, and apple slices. Attach some apple slices in a vertical or slanted position for more visual interest. Glue one apple slice hori-zontally over the top of the arrangement. Fill in any gaps with the lichen, secured in place with hot glue. Place candle cup on top of arrangement by pressing spike into top. Add a candle to complete the arrangement.

WINTER FRUIT ARRANGEMENT

MATERIALS:

One 5x6-inch-diameter green-glazed ceramic pot with domed top

Plastic foam cut to fit pot

2-3 dried pomegranates

10-12 dried bay leaves

8-10 cinnamon sticks

1 bunch red pepperberries

Spanish moss

Handful large lichen pieces

Glue gun/glue sticks

STEP 1

With hot glue, secure plastic foam in pot.

STEP 2

With hot glue, secure a thick mat of moss to domed top. Allow tendrils of moss to overlap edges.

STEP 3

With ample amounts of hot glue, secure pomegranates to moss. Secure lichen pieces between fruit and moss. Group sprigs of berries, evenly distributed, on moss. Use hot glue to secure in place.

STEP 4

With hot glue, tuck bay leaves into arrangement around fruit and berries. Secure cinnamon sticks into arrangement, distributing evenly.

This arrangement can be scented by adding a few drops of cinnamon oil to mossed areas.

SCENTS TO SIMMER

First impressions set the mood for things to come. Place a simmering pot near the entry hall to welcome guests with delicious aromas. Experiment with spices, herbs, and oils to create your own delightful scents. Leaves and clippings of aromatic materials left over from craft projects can be saved to mix and simmer. When herbs become a bit too stale for cooking, add them to a simmering pot. Simmers can be freshened by adding similar ingredients and topping the heated pot with boiling water. Discard after four or five uses.

Making a simmer is extremely easy. Place all ingredients in the top section of a simmering pot, candle-heated or electric. Add boiling water to fill. Place simmering pot over heat source. Add more boiling water as needed.

Apple Vanilla Simmer

½ teaspoon ground nutmeg

1 tablespoon whole cloves

4 broken cinnamon sticks

1 tablespoon vanilla

8 drops apple-scented oil

Orange Spice Simmer

¼ cup dried or fresh orange peel

1 tablespoon whole cloves

2 pieces broken cinnamon stick

8 drops sweet orange oil

Pine Forest Simmer

¼ cup dried pine needles

¼ cup dried cedar or similar evergreen needles

6-8 small cones

1 tablespoon whole cloves

8-10 drops pine oil

May Your Christmas be a Happy One And may the New Year bring You Contentment and Prosperity in overflowing measure.

ROSE PETAL WREATH

The sweetness of the summer rose is evoked when the moist potpourri is opened and perfumes of May fill the air. December is the time for scarlet petals and boughs of green, a brilliant finale to the year.

MATERIALS:

One 8-inch-diameter straw wreath

1 bunch preserved evergreens

1 bunch preserved boxwood

Generous handful purple dried miniature rosebuds

½ cup miniature red rose petals

12 small sprigs baby's breath

22 inches of 2-inch-wide fine, stiff brass mesh

7 inches florist's wire

Spray adhesive

Newspaper

Glue gun/glue sticks

STEP 1

With hot glue, secure greenery to front and sides of wreath (see page 39). With hot glue, attach miniature rosebuds to wreath, distributing evenly. Intersperse small sprigs of baby's breath among the greenery and rosebuds.

STEP 2

Move wreath to a well-ventilated area and place on newspaper. Cover lightly with spray adhesive. Sprinkle rose petals over wreath.

STEP 3

Tie a single bow of gold mesh, 5 inches wide overall, with 3 ½-inch streamers (see page 33). Finish streamers in an inverted V shape. To form hanger, push wire through straw at center point of wreath back. Twist wire ends together to form a loop.

Christmas joy is in my heart

BRIGHT BRASS SACHETS

A most unlikely place to find a beautiful material for crafting is in the plumbing department of the hardware store. Fine brass mesh is used for fitting drains as strainers. The mesh is available in several gauges and is flexible. Light-gauge mesh can be cut with scissors or pinking shears. This sheet of mesh can be used to make angel wings or fashioned into beautiful bows.

PLEATED BRASS SACHET

MATERIALS:

6 ¼x12-inch piece brass mesh screen

½ yard 1 ½-inch-wide iridescent purple-and-gold organdy ribbon

Handful potpourri

STEP 1

Place mesh on flat work surface. Fold over ¼ inch of the shorter sides and flatten.

STEP 2

Form pleats along the 12-inch sides by folding the mesh back and forth onto itself.

STEP 3

Fold pleated mesh in half, with the ¼-inch folds turned inward. Align sides and fold these edges over twice.

STEP 4

Fill bag with potpourri. Gather mesh 2 ½ inches from top. Make a pretty single bow with ribbon. Fan pleats out above the bow.

STEP 5

Flatten sachet bottom by pressing sachet down on work surface.

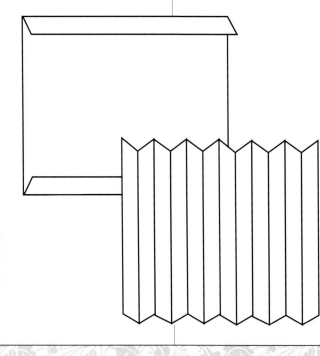

CANDLESTICK WREATH

MATERIALS:

Three 12-inch pieces green craft or florist's wire

6 sprigs preserved evergreens

6 sprigs preserved boxwood

1 yard of ¼-inch-wide fine, stiff gold mesh

Wire cutter

Glue gun/glue sticks

STEP 1

Using wire, form a 5-inch-diameter circle by twisting wire ends together.

STEP 2

With hot glue, attach greenery to wire wreath base. Be sure to cover completely. Secure some greenery on top of other sprigs to give wreath a full appearance.

STEP 3

Twist gold-mesh strip around a pencil to form curls. With hot glue, secure to greenery, pulling curls out to vary pattern. Place wreath over Rose-Petaled Candlestick.

PETALED SACHET

MATERIALS:

8x8-inch square fine, brass mesh

11 inches of ½-inch-wide gold mesh

Handful potpourri

Scissors

STEP 1

Finish ends of 11-inch strip in an inverted V shape. Set aside. Fold edges of 8x8-inch square over ¼ inch and flatten. Bring corners of mesh square up to form a pouch shape. Bottom should be 3 inches wide. Pull pointed edges out to flatten slightly and give a petal effect.

STEP 2

Fill with potpourri. To finish, wrap strip around sachet.

SCALLOPED SACHET

MATERIALS:

One 8-inch-diameter circle of brass mesh, edges scalloped

One 8x¾-inch rectangle brass mesh

Handful potpourri

STEP 1

Place potpourri in center of brass-mesh circle. Gather mesh circle up around potpourri.

STEP 2

Fold the mesh rectangle in thirds lengthwise. Tie around gather on mesh sachet.

ROSE-PETALED CANDLESTICK

MATERIALS:

One 5 ½-inch porcelain or wooden pedestal candlestick

Generous handful dried rose petals

White craft glue

Small bowl

Water with a few drops of rose oil to moisten hands

STEP 1

Place rose petals in bowl. Cover candlestick with white craft glue and place upright in bowl. Moisten hands with rose water. With hands, apply rose petals to candlestick. Press petals into glue. Cover all areas completely. Allow glue to set completely (usually four to five hours).

STEP 2

Place wreath over candlestick.

CHRISTMAS SACHET ORNAMENT

MATERIALS:

8 inches of 5-inch-wide provincial-print border fabric

8 inches of ¼-inch-wide satin burgundy ribbon

Handful potpourri

Coordinating thread and needle

STEP 1

Place border fabric, right side up, on flat work surface. Sew a ¼-inch hem along top edge. Fold fabric in half lengthwise. Using a ¼-inch seam allowance, stitch these edges together.

STEP 2

Position fabric with seam centered and facing upward. Using a ¼-inch seam allowance, sew bottom edge to create a bag.

Turn top edge under ¼ inch and hem.

STEP 3

Turn bag right side out. Stuff with potpourri. Encircle bag with ribbon and make a single bow ½ inch from top edge.

HERBAL ANGELS

MATERIALS FOR ONE ANGEL:

One 4-inch wooden doll with wooden bead head, dowel with bead arms, and legs

7 inches of 3-inch-wide provincial-print border fabric

Small amount of a botanical for angel hair

Small amount of a botanical for angel shoes

2 large bay leaves

Small scraps of ribbon, berries, and botanicals

1 small basket or a wreath made from a circle of twine

Coordinating thread and needle

Small scissors

Straight pins

Iron

White craft glue

Glue gun/glue sticks

STEP 1

Assemble doll if necessary. Place fabric piece, right side down, on work surface. Turn top edge down ¼ inch and press or pin into place. Sew a running stitch to secure. Push fabric along thread to gather. Place gather around doll's neck before knotting fabric. Adjust if necessary. Knot, trimming excess thread. A ¼-inch hem may be stitched, or fabric can be left slightly frayed.

STEP 2

Hold gathered fabric around angel's neck. With scissors, make two small slits for armholes approximately ¼ inch below gather. Pull arms through holes.

STEP 3

Pull fabric around back until it overlaps ¼ inch. Secure overlap with hot glue to form a seam.

STEP 4

With hot glue, attach small botanicals for hair to doll's head. With white craft glue, attach botanicals for shoes or acorn caps to doll's feet.

STEP 5

Use hot glue and scraps of ribbon and botanicals to decorate dress and neckline. With hot glue, attach a basket or wreath to doll's hand.

STEP 6

Use hot glue to attach bay leaves to doll's back to form angel wings.

LIST OF SUGGESTED BOTANICALS FOR ANGEL HAIR

Baby's breath, Bleached maidenhair fern, Calendula petals, Feverfew, Gold yarrow, Lichen, Miniature rosebud petals, Sea lavender, Small white globe amaranth, Spanish moss, Star flowers, Sweet annie, Yellow statice

LIST OF SUGGESTED BOTANICALS FOR ANGEL SHOES

Acorn caps, Calendula petals, Ground cinnamon, Ground thyme, Lichen, Red rose petals, Small preserved green leaves, Sphagnum moss

Christmas morning finds us gathered round the tree amid ribbons and wrappings. Gifts crafted from a garden lovingly tended evoke summer days past and spring days to come. In this and every season, find joy in the garden, and find joy in the giving.

HERBAL TWIG TREE

During winter months, when branches are frosty and the garden sleeps under a blanket of snow, herbal plants wait for spring to come. Often rosemary will still yield a few green stems, but for the other herbs needed to make an herbal twig tree, a trip to the grocery store or health-food shop may be in order. The base of this tree was purchased, as the knobby kiwi vines needed are rarely found in a home garden. Any branches or vines may be substituted. This tree is crafted with fresh herbs that will stay fresh-looking for several days. Herbs will then dry in place.

MATERIALS:

One 20-inch twig tree base (see next page)

1 bunch sweet annie

1 bunch rosemary

1 bunch mint

1 bunch red or pink heather

1 bunch oregano

24-28 acorn clusters

Sphagnum moss

15-18 small Christmas tree candle cups, remove clip mechanism

15-18 small red Christmas candles to fit cups

Plant mister

Glue gun/glue sticks

STEP 1

Place all fresh materials with freshly cut ends in water for two hours to allow stems a good drink before adding to tree.

STEP 2

Fill kitchen sink or large mixing bowl with cool water. Soak approximately five handfuls of moss for five minutes. Drain excess liquid and pack moss around center cylinder of tree between twigs.

STEP 3

Gently push stems of fresh botanicals into wet moss, distributing evenly. Using plant mister, spray leaves.

STEP 4

Use hot glue to attach acorn clusters to twigs, distributing evenly. Glue candle clips to twig ends, distributing evenly. Place candles in candle cups.

CHRISTMAS TWIG TREE BASE

MATERIALS:

One 6-inch-diameter clay pot

One 6-inch-diameter round plastic foam block cut to fit pot

9x20-inch piece lightweight chickenwire

125-130 twigs, graduated in size from 5 to 10 inches

Sphagnum moss

Florist's pins

Florist's spool wire

Wire cutter

Garden clippers

Glue gun/glue sticks

STEP 1

Lay the chicken wire on a flat surface. Place a thick strip of moss lengthwise on center of wire. Bend wire sides together to form a cylinder tightly filled with moss. Press sides together to secure. Using florist's wire, wind wire around entire length of cylinder to secure. Cut wire with wire cutter. Push end into moss.

STEP 2

With hot glue, secure plastic foam in pot. Center open end of cylinder on foam. With florist's pins, secure cylinder base to plastic foam by looping pin through chicken-wire holes. Push pin ends into foam. Use a large quantity of hot glue around cylinder base to secure. Add more glue as needed. Cover foam with moss, secured in place with hot glue.

STEP 3

Beginning at cylinder base and working upward, push larger twigs through holes in wire and well into moss. Secure in place with hot glue where branches touch wire. Continue process, using smaller twigs closer to the top to achieve a pine-tree shape. Space twigs as evenly as possible. With garden clippers, trim twig ends as needed to form a more perfectly shaped tree. Press additional moss through branches around cylinder to cover wire and glued areas.

Candles on Herbal Twig Tree were lit for photography. Small candles burn down within 10 minutes. Should you choose to light candles on this project, never leave them unattended and have a water source or fire extinguisher at hand. Use extreme caution with all candles during the holidays, especially when young children are present. Always check your local fire ordinances to determine if candles may be burned on a tree.

STOCKING SACHET

MATERIALS:

One 14x6½-inch-wide provincial-print border fabric

6 ½ inches moss-green trim with tassels

Small amount dried cedar

8 small red berries

1 dried miniature rose stem

Large handful potpourri

Tracing paper

Pencil

Coordinating thread and needle

Iron

Straight pins

Scissors

Glue gun/glue sticks

STEP 1

Transfer pattern to tracing paper and cut out. Fold border fabric in half, right sides together. Pin pattern to fabric and cut out.

STEP 2

With right sides together, stitch around stocking sides ¼ inch from edge. Leave stocking top open. Fold ¼ inch of the top of stocking down and press well. Turn stocking right side out and press.

STEP 3

Fill stocking with potpourri. Stitch opening closed. With hot glue, secure trim around top edge of stocking. Attach greens and berries to the stocking front with hot glue.

SPICY WINTER POTPOURRI

½ cup allspice

½ cup caraway seeds

½ cup cardamon seeds

1 cup star anise

1 cup cinnamon stick pieces

½ cup dried rosehips

½ cup rosemary

½ ounce cinnamon powder

2 tablespoons orrisroot

6 drops cinnamon oil

2 drops lavender

Crockery bowl

To make potpourri, see instructions on page 44.

CHRISTMAS PURSE SACHET

MATERIALS:

15 inches of 4-inch-wide provincial-print border fabric

19 inches red cotton seam piping

14 inches of $^1/_{16}$-inch-wide red grosgrain ribbon

One $^5/_8$-inch wooden bead

8 inches of $^1/_2$-inch red French wired ribbon

Coordinating thread and needle

Straight pins

Iron

Glue gun/glue sticks

STEP 1

Measure 2 inches from one end of fabric strip. Cut end into a V shape. Fold edges of V shape under and hem.

STEP 2

Fold opposite end over to within $^1/_2$-inch of the end of the V shape. Cut a second V shape on folded end. Set top aside.

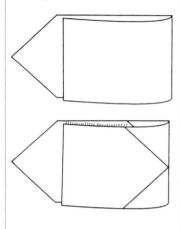

STEP 3

Place fabric right side up. Align raw edge of piping with edge of fabric. Pin in place with straight pins. Stitch piping into place.

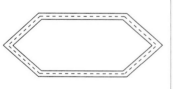

STEP 4

Place second fabric piece facedown on piped fabric piece. Sew pieces together.

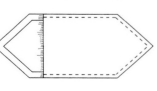

STEP 5

Turn pouch right side out. Fold triangular pointed end over opening. Press well with warm iron.

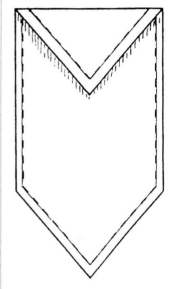

STEP 6

Sew narrow red ribbon to pouch beneath fold. Fill with potpourri and secure fold in place with hot glue.

STEP 7

Using wired ribbon, cover bead. With hot glue, attach bead to folded V shape. Trim ribbon end in an inverted V shape.

PATCHWORK SACHET

MATERIALS:

Four 3x3-inch squares provincial-print Christmas fabric

One 2x2-inch square provincial-print fabric to coordinate

½ yard ⅛-inch-wide gold trim

4 inches of ½-inch-wide deep red French wired ribbon

Balsam

Cotton batting

1 blank button cover

Coordinating thread and needle

Scissors

Wire cutter

Glue gun/glue sticks

STEP 1

Place 3x3-inch fabric squares together. With sharp scissors, cut in half along the diagonal. Sew one triangle of each fabric together to form a square. Sew the remaining four triangles together to form a square.

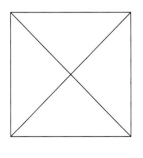

STEP 2

With right sides together, stitch the two squares together. Leave a 2-inch opening. Turn right side out and stuff with balsam and batting. Stitch opening closed.

STEP 3

Use 2-inch square of fabric to cover button cover, following manufacturer's instructions.

STEP 4

Gather one edge of wired ribbon and pull tightly (see page 33). Use wire cutter to trim excess wire. Fan out ribbon circle. Glue ends together to form a seam. With hot glue, attach ribbon circle to underside of button cover.

STEP 5

With hot glue, secure trim around edges of sachet and button cover. Glue button cover to center of sachet.

HERBAL CHRISTMAS ORNAMENT

MATERIALS:

One 3 ½-inch-diameter plastic foam ball

1 handful crushed Spanish moss or lichen

15 spikes dried lavender

4 small sprigs red pepperberries

8 small sprigs artemisia

6 dried rosehips

4 small dried rose leaves

4 small bunches berries

Assorted bits of greenery

Pine essential oil

10 inches red cording

White craft glue

Glue gun/glue sticks

STEP 1

Place crushed moss in a bowl. Cover plastic foam ball with craft glue and roll in moss to cover. Allow glue to set before proceeding. Fold cording in half and knot edges together. Turn ends under and glue knot to top of ball.

STEP 2

With hot glue, secure the rose leaves around cord approximately 1 inch from knot. With hot glue, attach the tips of lavender spikes to the ball between the leaves. Attach pepperberries on top of leaves. Attach remaining berries next to pepperberries. Secure rosehips near cording and scattered over top of ornament. Use artemisia as filler. Place a few drops of pine oil on mossy areas of ornament.

RESOURCE GUIDE

Adhesives

BLACK & DECKER
Thermogrip Glue Gun
Hot & low-melt glue guns

LOCTITE CORPORATION
4450 Cranwood Parkway
Cleveland, OH 44128
(800) 321-9188
Wide range of adhesives

Air-dry Modeling Clay

BINNIE & SMITH
Consumer Information
1100 Church Street
P.O. Box 431
Easton, PA 18004
Model Magic

Baskets & Wreaths

COMFORTS OF HOME
(800) 44-SMELL
Scented twig products

Decorative Accessories

EL PLATO
1736 18th Street
San Francisco, CA 94107
(415) 621-4487
Glassware and giftware

HANDCRAFT OF SOUTH TEXAS
Route 3, Box 73
Pharr, TX 78577
(210) 781-6165
Wire heart-shaped wreath

WISTERIA ANTIQUES
5870 Soquel Drive
Soquel, CA 95073
(408) 462-2900
French antiques

Candle-making Supplies

BRUSHY MOUNTAIN BEE FARM, INC.
Rt. 1 Box 135
Moravian Falls, NC 28654
(919) 921-3640
Pure beeswax, molds

Dried/Preserved Botanicals

COAST
149 Morris Street
San Francisco, CA 94107
(800) 562-3681
Full range of dried/preserved botanicals

CRAMER'S POSIE PATCH
740 High Ridge Road
Columbia, PA 17512
(717) 684-0777
Dried botanical wreaths also

THE GALVESTON WREATH COMPANY
1124 25th Street
Galveston, TX 77550
(800) 874-8597

HOLLAND DRIED FLOWERS, LTD.
205 Champagne Drive, Unit 3
Downsview, Ontario,
CANADA M3J 2C3
Wholesale only, no mail order

JONES & BONES, UNLTD.
621 Capitola Avenue
Capitola, CA 95010
(408) 462-0521
Gourmet herbs

TAPESTRIES OF NATURE
8N191 Grand Arbor
Maple Park, IL 60151
(708) 365-2416
Dried flowers

WEAVER'S DRIED FLOWERS & HERBS
Rt. 1, Box 178A
Easton, MO 64443
(816) 253-9182
Freeze-dried fruits also

WILD BOTANICALS
P.O. Box 2264
Corvallis, OR 97339
(503) 929-6492
Dried & fresh botanicals

KNUD NIELSEN COMPANY, INC.
P.O. Box 746
Evergreen, AL 36401

NATURALLY YOURS
1423 Buckskin Drive
Santa Maria, CA 93454
(805) 922-6184
Freeze-dried flowers

VAL'S NATURALS, INC.
Attn: Valerie Hatcher
P.O. Box 832
Kathleen, FL 33849-0832
(813) 858-8991
Miniature rosebuds, melaleuca leaves & pepperberries

European Specialties

D. BLUMCHEN & COMPANY
P.O. Box 929
Maywood, NJ 07607
Extraordinary items

Fabric

BENARTEX, INC.
1412 Broadway
New York, NY 10018
(212) 840-3250

ROBERT KAUFMAN CO., INC.
Box 59266
Greenmead Station
Los Angeles, CA 90059-0266
(800) 877-2066

PIERRE DEUX FRENCH COUNTRY
Three Pine Inn
Ocean Avenue
P.O. Box 996
Carmel, CA 93921
(408) 624-8185
Provincial-print fabric borders

Garden Accessories

THE BRITISH ACCENT
18 West Lake Street
Poughkeepsie, NY 12601
(800) 487-7855
Fine & unusual home & garden products

Garden Tools

FISKARS MANUFACTURING CORPORATION
7811 West Stewart Avenue
Wausau, WI 54401
Excellent garden tools

Notions

SULKY OF AMERICA
3113-D Broadpoint Drive
Harbor Heights, FL 33983
Thread & iron-on transfer pens

WALLFLOWER DESIGNS
1573 Millersville Road
Millersville, MD 21108
Fabric markers

Paint

ACCENT PRODUCTS DIVISION
HPPG, Borden Inc.
Lake Zurich, IL 60047
All colors, metallics & glue

Papermaking

CARRIAGE HOUSE HANDMADE PAPER WORKS
P.O. Box 197
North Hatfield, MA 01066
(800) 669-8781
Catalog available

Paper Products

THE GIFTED LINE
700 Larkspur Landing Circle
Suite 163
Larkspur, CA 94939
Victorian papers

LAURA STEIN DESIGN
P.O. Box 1226
Avalon, CA 90704
(310) 510-9622
Paper lace doilies & nosegay holders

Plants & Seeds

BERRY HILL HERB GARDEN
Box 95 RR1
Old Keene Road
Walpole, N.H. 03608

BLUESTONE PERENNIALS
7211 Middle Ridge Road
Madison, OH 44057

BOUNTIFUL GARDENS ECOLOGY ACTION
5798 Ridgewood Road
Willits, CA 95490

BUSSE GARDENS
Route 2 Box 238
Cokato, MN 55321

J.L. HUDSON, SEEDSMAN
P.O. Box 1058
Redwood City, CA 94064

PARKS SEED FLOWERS AND VEGETABLES
Cokesbury Road
Greenwood, SC 29647

PINE TREE GARDEN SEEDS
New Gloucester, ME 04260

THE COOK'S GARDEN
P.O. Box 535
Londonberry, VT 05148

THE NATURAL GARDEN
38W 443 Highway 64
St. Charles, IL 60175

THE SANDY MUSH HERB NURSERY
Route 2 Surrett Cove Road
Leicester, NC 28748

THE THYME GARDEN
20546 Alsea Highway
Alsea, OR 97324

THOMPSON & MORGAN, INC.
P.O. Box 1308
Jackson, NJ 08527

WILLOW OAK
Flower & Herb Farm
8109 Telegraph Road
Severn, MD 21144

Potpourri Supplies

BALSAM FIR PRODUCTS
Morse Hill Road
P.O. Box 9
West Paris, ME 04289
Balsam

BONNY DOON FARM
600 Martin Road
Santa Cruz, CA 95060
Lavender & oils, brochure available

HANNA'S POTPOURRI
SPECIALTIES, INC.
P.O. Box 3647
Fayetteville, AK 72702
(800) 327-9826
Oils & potpourri

HERB GARDEN
FRAGRANCES
3744 Section Road
Cincinnati, OH 45236
Blended oils

HERB HOUSE CATALOG
340 Grove Street
Bluffton, OH 45817
(419) 358-7189

THE HERB &
SPICE COLLECTION
P.O. Box 118
Norway, IA 52318-0118
(800) 365-4372
Potpourri supplies

HOVE PARFUMEUR, LTD.
824 Royal Street
New Orleans, LA 70116
(504) 525-7827
Oils & potpourri kits

KIEHL'S
109 Third Avenue
New York, NY 10003
Essential oils

LIBERTY NATURAL
PRODUCTS
8120 SE Stark Street
Portland, OR 97216
(800) 289-8427
Oils

LORANN OILS
4518 Aurelius Road
P.O. Box 22009
Lansing, MI 48909-2009
(800) 248-1302
Scented oils

MEADOWSWEET
HERB FARM
729 Mount Holly Road
Shrewsbury, VT 05738
(802) 492-3565

MRS. O'QUINN'S
SCENT SHOPPE
1908 Joanne Street
Wichita, KS 67203
(316) 943-2585
Essential and perfumed oils

RAVEN'S NEST
4539 Iroquois Trail
Duluth, GA 30136
(404) 242-3901
Herbal & scented oils

SAN FRANCISCO HERB CO.
250 14th Street
San Francisco, CA 94103
Scented oils & botanicals

SUMERU
"A blend of heaven and earth"
P.O. Box 2110
Freedom, CA 95019
(408) 722-4104
Potpourri and essential oils

Pottery

ALBION ANTIQUES &
GARDENS
1496 East Valley Road
Santa Barbara, CA 93108
(805) 969-3803

Pressed Flowers & Herbs

TOM THUMB WORKSHOPS
Route 13, P.O. Box 382
Mappsville, VA 23407
(804) 824-3507
Pressed flowers, herbs,
oils & accessories

Ribbon & Trim

CREATIVE BEGINNINGS
475 Morro Bay Blvd.
Morro Bay, CA 93442
(800) 642-7238
Victorian charms

ELSIE'S ESQUISIQUES
208 State Street
P.O. Box 260
St. Joseph, MI 49085
(800) 742-SILK
Austrian trims, antique ribbons

JHB INTERNATIONAL
Denver, CO 80231
Buttons

PAULETTE KNIGHT
343 Vermont Street
San Francisco, CA 94102
French wired ribbon

LION RIBBON COMPANY, INC.
100 Metro Way
P.O. Box 1548
Secaucus, NJ 07096
Wired ribbon

MIDORI, INC.
3827 Stone Way North
Seattle, WA 98103
(206) 547-9553

Statuary

CARRUTH STUDIO, INC.
1178 Farnsworth Road
Waterville, OH 43566
(419) 878-3060

FLORENTINE
CRAFTSMEN, INC.
46-24 28th Street
Long Island City, NY 11101
(800) 876-3567
Delightful garden sculptures

O'BRIEN IRONWORKS
1760 Monrovia Avenue B-3
Costa Mesa, CA 92627
(714) 646-3290
Wonderful iron urns &
garden furniture

Wood Products

ADD YOUR TOUCH
P.O. Box 570
Ripon, WI 54971
(414) 748-6777
Birdhouses, small wood
products

DESIGNS BY
BENTWOOD, INC.
P.O. Box 1676
Thomasville, GA 31799
Baskets & boxes

WALNUT HOLLOW
FARM WOODCRAFT
STORE
Hwy. 23 North
Dodgeville, WI 53533
(800) 950-5101

INDEX

Joni Prittie